BRUCE G. McWILLIAMS'

UNDER-33
FINANCIAL PLAN

BRUCE G. McWILLIAMS'

UNDER-33 FINANCIAL PLAN:

Four Painless Steps to Lifelong Prosperity

BRUCE G. McWILLIAMS

dp

DELACORTE PRESS/NEW YORK

Published by
Delacorte Press
The Bantam Doubleday Dell Publishing Group, Inc.
1 Dag Hammarskjold Plaza
New York, New York 10017

Manufactured in the United States of America

First printing

Library of Congress Cataloging in Publication Data
McWilliams, Bruce G.
    Bruce G. McWilliams' under-33 financial plan.

    Includes bibliographical references.
    1. Finance, Personal.   2. Investments.   I. Title.
II. Title: Under-33 financial plan.
HG179.M39   1988   332.024   87-27151
ISBN 0-385-29617-7

This work is lovingly dedicated to:

My Parents, for almost 33 years; my friends,
and
Maryanne,

my sometime editor and full-time solace
during this seemingly unending task

Contents

An Acknowledgment   ix

Introduction   xi

Section A Plan   1
   1. Young, Professional, and Broke   3
   2. Why Do You Want So Much Money?   14
   3. The Risks and the Rewards   25
   4. Make a Plan. Period.   33

Section B Budget   57
   5. Save Creatively   59
   6. De-Taxing   86

Section C Home Purchase   95
   7. The First Step: Buy Your Home   97
   8. Getting Mortgage Money   111

Section D Invest   131
   9. Walking Down Wall Street: Stocks and Bonds   133
      Appendix: The Risky Business of Options   154
   10. Hitting the Home Run: Mutual Funds   162
   11. The Mutual Fund for You   178
   12. Reap!   196

An Acknowledgment

After my first book, I felt a great responsibility to thank those who had expressly helped me with the book itself. On completing this, my second work, I now realize that my ability to write a book results from a lifetime of learning from friends and teachers. The specific words put down on these pages are a synthesis of that learning. With that in mind, I have a great debt to pay. Though this list is far from complete, it came to mind one dark and rainy day in New York City. It is alphabetical.

Also included in the list are the names of those whose stories are included in the text. Some were friends before the work began and some became friends by agreeing to open their financial souls to the world. I promised anonymity, and hence their names and sometimes their sex and location have been changed to respect this agreement. Thank you all.

Marilyn Abraham, Ricki Berman, Ann and Bill Boucher, Edward Bowman, Cathy Calto, Judy Davidoff, Janet Kreisberg Evanczuk, Kevin Finnegan, Kathy Gordon, Maurine Gordon, Richard Kass, Henrick Kibak, Susanne Kibak, Ann Scott Knight, Randlett Lawrence, Carol Ramsey Lintz, Gary Luke, David and Miriam Mitchell, Paul Mitchell and Vickey La Motte, Steve Morton, Peyton Moss, R. Parameswaran, Paul Ponzo, Dana Priest,

Bruce Jordan Roberts, Tom and Sophie Seale, Charlie and Annie Stebbins, Martin Steinman, Charolette and Hugh Thurschwell, and Cory and Kris Yulinski.

Disclaimer

I am not an SEC-registered investment adviser or a registered representative or a Certified Financial Planner. I have owned and continue to own some of the securities mentioned in the text. The opinions about securities should not be construed as recommendations. I do not know your particular financial position and the securities and strategies may not be appropriate. As I make clear in the study, the past performance of these securities is not an indication of their future direction.

Introduction

I graduated from the Wharton Business School in 1984 and settled into what I thought was a high-paying job with Citibank in New York City. I soon discovered that if I was ever going to get anywhere financially, I couldn't rely on my salary alone. I talked to various financial planners and read financial planning books; this proved disappointing. The financial planners only wanted to sell me investment products and the financial planning books gave me so many choices that I was left pretty much where I began.

I set out to put together my own financial plan for men and women, single or married, who were under the age of thirty-three, and earned between $20,000 and $60,000 per year. This book is the result of that research. I talked with young people. I learned how they solved very common dilemmas, e.g., raising money for the down payment on a house. Everyone in our age group except those with trust funds and those with parents named Rockefeller shares the problem of how to get on the financial highway. What follows is a cogent program that puts these ideas to work.

You have in your hands a powerful tool. My plan is specific. I tell you what to do. Of course you'll have to tailor the plan to your own situation. I will provide you with the backbone for charting your financial course. The plan you are about to read was devised by me and, of course, any shortcomings are completely my own doing.

BRUCE G. McWILLIAMS'

UNDER-33
FINANCIAL PLAN

SECTION

 PLAN

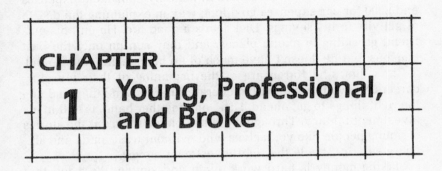

CHAPTER 1
Young, Professional, and Broke

Twenty-five-year-old Chris Remington smiled knowingly in his Brooklyn condo. The mirror-image condominium next door had just sold for $130,000. He and his best friend and roommate, Jim Dorian, had bought their condo only a year ago for $110,000 with a 10 percent, $11,000, down payment. In essence, the young partnership had already netted $20,000 on an $11,000 investment. That's a 182 percent return in just one year, a terrific investment in anybody's book.

Karen Gill left the University of Denver in 1979 and found a $10,000-per-year job researching the commercial real estate market in Dallas. By 1986—over the course of seven years—she had purchased two condominiums and picked up a piece of the action in two apartment buildings. She's had to take on partners, but that's the name of her game.

Dick Nofziger lives in Marina Del Rey, the singles' section of Los Angeles. The twenty-six-year-old engineer cruises in his Mazda RX-7 to the aerospace manufacturer TRW, where he works. A smart guy, Dick has received several degrees in engineering from UC Berkeley and currently earns a salary in the low $40's. Based on his low level of savings, though, you wouldn't know that his salary places him in the upper reaches of American wage earners. A paltry $800 resides in his savings and investment account. Twelve hundred dollars in monthly apartment expenses and $600 for car expenses go a long way in explaining the dearth of activity in his savings. Dick leads a good life. He and his girlfriend go skiing in exotic places, and they sun on only the best beaches. But he doesn't have much of an investment story to tell.

Chris, Jim, and Karen are at the beginning of their investing careers. They all began with moderate salaries. And they're doing the right things to get ahead. Dick, on the other hand, is still in his investment infancy. Throughout this book we'll look at the stories of young people like yourselves who, without trust funds and six-figure salaries, made the right investment moves.

Making money is hard work, plain and simple. It's a job that requires thought, patience, and diligence. The work doesn't require any great intellect, and in fact some Ph.D.'s I've known are notoriously bad at financial planning. But it does require more work than just standing in line for an hour waiting to buy a Lotto ticket.

THE PLAN: No Lotto

This book is for those of you who don't depend on the state lotteries to get ahead. It's for those who want to learn how to develop a sizable nest egg. We'll explore the investment menu and examine how to make those important choices. We'll explain the nuts and bolts of buying a house (and how you can raise the money for a down payment a lot quicker than you think). We'll talk about ways to cut your taxes and to put that money to more productive uses. We'll describe how to save your money in investment vehicles that are both safe *and* rewarding.

And, most important, we'll discuss ways to think about your money, how to cut your spending, and what to do with your investment returns. But you do have to know how to think about risk as well as reward, a subject we'll pick up shortly.

If you're like most young people whom I've spoken to and helped, I can guarantee you will increase your spendable income by at least 20 percent and your asset base—the nest egg—by at least 50 percent. Your spendable income is the amount of money you have at your discretion after paying taxes, while your asset base refers to investments you own: your savings account, your stock portfolio, your house, and so on. This translates to a 40 percent return on your financial investment, your creative capital, and your time. And that's not bad:

$$\frac{\text{Spendable Income} + 20\%}{\text{Asset Base} + 50\%} = \frac{+40\% \text{ Return on}}{\text{Investment}}$$

My plan is simple and consists of only four easy steps. It is targeted specifically at people of your age. Success with the plan doesn't rely on a killing in stock-index options, nor does it require a Ph.D. in mathematical finance to comprehend. To succeed with my plan requires foresight, thought, effort, a little creativity, and a lot of determination.

The Overriding Strategy

Staying away from schemes and worthless investments is critical. The state lottery is a ridiculous investment because the return offered hardly compensates for the microscopic odds of winning. Similarly, a promised 100 percent return from worm farms or some mail-order schemes is just as foolhardy.

Every so often the worm-farm scheme pops up. In it, hapless investors send money and, several weeks later, receive a package of baby worms. Instructions are included on how to turn your house, apartment, or garage into an actual worm farm. When the toddlers have grown into full-scale worms, you simply sell them off and reap the benefits. The promoter promises an eager market, but have you ever tried to sell worms? Needless to say, the only ones who win with these investments are the promoters.

I hope to steer you away from unpromising investments. That's the cornerstone of my strategy. That doesn't mean, however, that a 5 1/4 percent passbook savings account is by any means a "smart" investment. While you won't lose your money in a bank, you're still not optimizing or making the most of available investments. A risky investment, just by being risky, isn't necessarily a dumb investment. Nor, by the same token, is a riskless investment a "smart" one. An informed investor understands the potential risk and return in any given investment. Period.

My overriding strategy will offer sense and order to your financial picture. You will get ahead. You won't be forced to live hand-to-mouth (a far more prevalent situation *and* strategy than many of us would care to admit). And it could make you rich.

FIRST STEP: Be Smart and Make a Plan

The first step is to be smart. And by "smart" I mean that you should think intelligently about your available funds and assets and where you should be placing them. I'll help you work out a plan. A plan means putting pencil to paper (or using a computer if you have one). This part will be fun for a night or two. After that it will be drudgery. The aim is to figure out (1) where you stand today, (2) where you want to be, financially speaking, tomorrow, and (3) the steps you must take to get there.

But where, financially, do you want to find yourself tomorrow?

In no small way, how you answer this question depends on your disposition toward money: Do you spend money freely or in a guarded manner? Developing a plan, though, is critical regardless of your inclination. You must sit down and think about how much money you have coming in and where it goes. It's far easier just to walk down to the cash machine and get out whatever you need for the next few days. The problem with this strategy (and it *is* a strategy!) is that it always catches up with you. Unless you plan. Lottery winners usually squander their money. The same holds true for those who inherit millions, unless they plan or hire someone to manage their money.

The other aspect of being smart and planning requires investigating where you put your money. Understanding the inherent riskiness of an investment before it's too late is critical. For example, if you consider a certain mutual fund, you must read the prospectus and watch the market to determine whether the price of the fund rides calmly despite tempestuous stock-market storms or whether it rises and falls with each wave.

When seeking out stockbrokers, find out whether they have ever been in trouble with the SEC or the state securities authorities. Find out how the previous clients of a real estate broker feel about the quality of services performed. Before spending your time—and money—attending a real estate lecture that extols the virtues of "nothing-down" real estate, see if you can locate others who have actually reaped the benefits of free real estate. Simple commonsense checking should be done.

While 98 percent of the people in the financial services industries are ethical, honest, and conscientious, there are a few bad apples. You've got enough to worry about in choosing investments, you shouldn't have to worry about whether your cash will end up in someone else's pocket—without your permission.

Being smart and planning also means not expecting dramatic results overnight. Getting ahead is a long process, one that never ends. Take your time, think things through, and don't make investment decisions on a whim. Think about how long it took for you to save the money in the first place. If a broker says "Buy now or you'll miss the opportunity," I say "Go ahead, miss the opportunity." There will always be another one tomorrow. And the next day. And the following day. You have time. You're in charge here. After all—it's your money. Don't be so quick to throw it away.

SECOND STEP: Make a Budget and Save Creatively

The second stage in the process is to budget. This is the active portion of the planning process. Because of the exercise with the plan, you'll know where you are now and where you want to go. It's time to effect those changes in your incomes and outflows. There isn't much you can do about increasing your income in the short term. "Boss, I want a raise, NOW!" usually doesn't work. You can curtail your spending, though. At the risk of sounding Ben

Franklin-ish, a penny saved, because of taxes, is worth more than a penny earned.

Budgeting turns out to be more important than you might first think. For that, I offer A LITTLE THEORY. When we earn money we have two basic choices: We can spend it or we can save it. Saving, as you'll learn, doesn't have to mean a passbook savings account. It just means placing your money in something that provides a return on investment.

Paying money to a health club, going out to eat, and making rent payments is spending. Making mortgage payments, putting money in a tax-free bond fund, or buying stocks is saving.

I argue that buying a painting, despite what the art dealer tells you, is spending: You'll put it on your wall, the years will go by, and you'll bequeath it to your children. While, of course, you have to eat, spending money on groceries and going out on the town don't generate a return on investment, i.e., it's spending. On the other hand, when you save money in any of the multitude of fashions that we'll explore later, you earn rewards in the future. That's why planning and budgeting are imperative.

You'll never get ahead on your salary alone. Period. You may be comfortable, and you may meet all your current needs, but you'll never get ahead. The secret, as you grow older, is to generate a larger and larger portion of your annual income from your return on investments, not your salary. And, as noted above, these things take time. To make this happen, though, you must save and invest today. Beginning today.

Michael K. Evans, a fine financial writer, came up with a juicy explanation for saving money, starting now, as he explained in a recent *Gentleman's Quarterly.** If you start now, you can retire with $10 million. Begin with, say, $1,000 when you graduate from college. Next, simply increase that amount through the magic of compound interest 10,000 fold. We'll learn about this magic in the chapter on saving.

If you start today with $1,000 and earn money at a 25 percent

* "Money," *Gentleman's Quarterly* (New York: Condé Nast Publications), June 1986, p. 106.

clip (that is, 25 percent per year), you could end up with the $10 million by the time you're sixty-five. However, if you wait until you're forty-five—when you might think it's about time to start saving some money—and invest $10,000 instead of $1,000—you'll end up with only a mere $1 million when you retire. Earning a 25 percent return on investment is no easy trick, yet, Evans argues, it can be accomplished with real estate investments. The point is that the earlier you begin saving, the better.

Let me give you another, perhaps more down-to-earth, example. If you buy shares in a mutual fund which invests in home mortgage securities (we'll look at these and all mutual funds in the mutual funds chapter), you might earn 12 percent. If you put $1,000 into such a fund, you'll earn $120 a year—before taxes. Assuming you're in a combined federal, state, and local tax bracket of 30 percent, that means you'll have an additional $84 in spendable income. Big deal. I live in New York City. That's hardly the tariff for a Broadway show for two. But that's today. If you forgo the show, eat at home, and continue to put $1,000 a year into that fund for ten years, you'll have $16,000, even though you shelled out only $10,000 (10 years @ $1,000 per year). Your return on investment amounts to $6,000. That would buy you several, if not many, evenings out. If you continue to let this pool grow, you'll earn as much as your salary. You could quit your job.

That is the reason being smart, budgeting, and saving are important. Smart financial planning will increase your investment returns to the point where they far outweigh your salary or earned income. You won't be forced to remain at your current job; you'll be living better; you can do whatever you like—like buying a new house.

THIRD STEP: Buy a Home

The third step in the program is to own your own house. Or condo. Or co-op. Without a doubt, this is critical to getting ahead: You have to buy a residence. We all live in the after-tax world. And the after-tax cost of living in a place that you own is, almost without exception, cheaper than the cost of living in the place you rent. Houses can be had. Even at your current salary. Again, though, you have to be smart about it. And for most of you, it won't happen tomorrow. You can buy a home, though, and I'll describe the mechanics for making this happen.

As one new homeowner put it, buying your own place allows you "to be free of apartment-house-beige walls and to build shelves where you want them."* The major impediment, I've found, has nothing to do with money: It's mental. Getting over the hump of making the decision to buy a house is the biggest problem. "It's such a commitment," you think. "It's so expensive," you worry. "It's such a responsibility," you fret. These fears will evaporate once you gain an understanding of just what exactly buying a house means.

We'll look at finding the "right" house for your financial station, at getting a bank to talk with you, at sorting out the mortgage options, and, finally, at going to contract. Getting over the mental barricade *is* the major challenge. And you can't even think about getting ahead financially unless you own your own real estate.

There are three reasons a home serves as the foundation for a solid financial plan. When you buy a home you'll need to take out a mortgage. Because of the beneficence of the federal government, you can deduct interest payments, which reduces your taxes.

The second benefit comes from the automatic increase in your equity. Your percentage of ownership in the house grows as you make your mortgage payments. And, as you build up equity, you can borrow against it for further investments.

Third, as the value of real estate appreciates, your invested funds, or "equity," move right along with it but at a heightened or "leveraged" rate. That's the real bonanza. If real estate values are increasing at 10 percent per year, the value of your equity appreciates at a more dramatic rate. That's because you, not the bank, get the benefit. I'll explain.

Let's say you've made a down payment of $10,000 for your home and it was originally valued at $100,000. When you sell, say,

* Ruth Fairchild Pomeroy, *Redbook's Guide to Buying Your First Home* (New York: Fireside Books, 1980), p. 10.

two years later, you'll receive $121,000 (10 percent property appreciation per year). You pay off your mortgage with the bank, approximately $88,000. You're left with $33,000 in your pocket. You started with $10,000, you paid $2,000 in principal through your mortgage payments, and voilà, you have an additional $21,000—a 175 percent return on your money, free and clear (see Chart 1):

CHART 1

	*Equity		Bank Loan		Total Value
On Purchase Date	$10,000	+	$90,000	=	$100,000
Two Years Later	$33,000	+	$88,000	=	$121,000

* Equity refers to your investment.

Ergo, the benefits of home ownership are threefold: You can cut your taxes; you can borrow against your home; and its value appreciates while you're just living there. None of these benefits comes to you when you rent. We'll delve into the mechanics and financial benefits of buying your home in Chapters 6 and 7.

FOURTH STEP: Invest!

The fourth and final stage is where you use your creativity. You've planned. You've gotten your income and expenses under control, and you've built up a substantial nest egg. You're no longer paying for the landlord's Florida vacations. Now comes the time when you have to figure out your best investment strategy.

For instance, if you like reading annual reports, talking with brokers, reading the business section every day, and staying on top of the market, buying and selling individual stocks may be for you. On the other hand, if you want to do a little investigation at the beginning and then let your investment ride, a mutual fund may be your best bet. Mutual funds are run by professional money managers who buy and sell stocks for the fund. If you have an inclination for ferreting out houses and condos in need of a little fixing up, then buying handyman real estate specials may be your best choice and you can forget the stock market. Your particular likes and dislikes will point you in the direction that you should follow.

No particular investment strategy, prima facie, will earn you more money than another. Every broker, every financial planner, every real estate broker, will tell you—either explicitly or implicitly—that they know the way, if you'll just follow their advice. But the truth is, each investment strategy might work and then again it might not. Investing your hard-earned money is tough business and shouldn't be taken lightly. Consider the following:

If you read real estate books in the early 1980s you would have discovered that real estate outperformed all other major investment categories in the 1970s.

If you took a graduate course in finance, you would learn that since the 1920s common equity—stocks—have yielded the best results, bar none.

The bond market in 1985 performed superlatively. If you bought metals, such as gold and silver, right before they took off in the mid-1970s and sold them when inflation began to subside, you would have found that precious metals were the best possible investment made.

Getting confused? Good. You can find arguments for and against virtually every stripe of investment. And most likely you can find academics of various shades to back up any contention you're likely to hear about a particular investment vehicle.

The two kinds of long-term investments that should be made by people at the beginning of their investing careers are real estate and common stocks: real estate because it offers safety, tax benefits, and solid returns; and mutual funds because they offer the best long-run returns with diversified risk and are easy to pick. At the conclusion of the book, though, you'll be able to choose for yourself what you think are the best investments for your income level, risk tolerance, and money propensity (your "money propensity" will be unveiled in the next chapter).

That's it—the four painless steps: Plan, save creatively, buy a home, and invest. Simple. Not really, but it's a lot less tortuous than you might think. There's no reason an intelligent young professional, almost regardless of income level, can't get on the financial steamship and push ahead.

At the end of this book you will have the tools and techniques for setting in motion a financially respectable plan to guide you through your life and to earn peace of mind. You'll control your financial resources—not the other way around. By conscientiously following the steps and suggestions:

- You'll have your spending under control,
- You'll be on the way to buying a house,
- You'll understand how to invest intelligently in the stock market,
- And, most important, you'll know that you can achieve your financial goals.

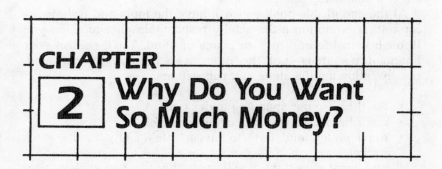

CHAPTER 2
Why Do You Want So Much Money?

Twenty-eight-year-old Caryn Reed is terribly interested in her money. She says, "I've always invested in stocks. My first jump into the market was in junior high school." She graduated from the University of California in economics and went straight into the Navy. By the time she got out of the armed services, six years later, she had saved or earned $100,000 from her investments. Despite the fact that Uncle Sam pays your room and board and you get to buy at a discount from the base exchange, the armed services is not known for killer salaries: Caryn earned $250 per week. However, she scrimped, she saved, and finally she invested in Florida real estate—not a swamp, but a single-family dwelling. During this time she continued to invest in the stock market.

Caryn and I were classmates in college. Whenever we met in the halls, the second words out of her mouth, after the perfunctory "How-ya-do'in?" consisted of a rundown of the performance of her stock portfolio. For one semester I knew the fortunes of Seagate Technology almost better than that of my own family. After the Navy, Caryn went to work for a mutual fund house where, after a short time, she was selected to manage one of the nation's largest mutual funds.

Caryn has always spent many of her waking hours thinking about money—thinking of ways to save it, earn it, and invest it. Most people are concerned with money. Rich people are people who are terribly concerned with *making* money. In this chapter we're going to talk about making money. This chapter will help you think about the issues involved in financial planning: goal setting and risk tolerance. At the end you'll fill out a questionnaire that will give us an indication of your desire to earn money, your Money Propensity. This sets the stage for the next chapter, when we actually choose goals that will make up your plan.

Money

Money is a funny subject. The energy we devote to getting it, how we treat it once we get it, how free we are with it, what we use it for, and why we want it in the first place all reveal aspects of our personalities.

I assume that since you bought this book you are (1) interested in money, (2) young, and (3) relatively unversed in the nuances of investing. You say, "But *who* isn't interested in money?" As I hope to prove to you, people who are interested in money spend their time trying to increase their wealth while those who aren't as interested spend little or no time at this endeavor.

You'll gain much information, and learn many tips and angles and several strategies, for generating more money and keeping it. More than that, though, long after the tips have dissipated into the lost recesses of your mind, I hope to provide you with an understanding of your own relationship to and with money. As the book unfolds I'll prescribe a framework, along with various strategies, that can and should be adopted, depending on your proclivities, your intent, and your fastidiousness about making money.

"Now wait a second," you say. "I'm as intent as the next guy on making money, a lot of it. I just want to know what to do to make the most." Fair enough; if you say that, then you're making a statement about your own feelings toward money. The strategy I present will, conceptually, earn you an ample, robust return.

How Much Money Do You Want?

Before setting off on this lucrative journey, we need to establish two critical matters: How much more money do you want and when do you want it? To make a plan requires knowing where you are today and where you're going. An open-ended plan, one that has no endpoint, will take you there: nowhere.

The best way to determine how much money you want is to figure out what you're going to do with it once you get it. As I've implored, and as I implore throughout the book, you need to buy a home. Once you've learned about prices in the local housing market, you can estimate how much you'll need to make a down payment. Do you have kids? You want to have enough money to send them to college. Perhaps this will be your long-term goal, to establish a plan that generates enough money to get them through college without bankrupting you.

The list of projects is endless. Maybe you'd like to boast of a vacation home within five years. That's something to shoot for. Or you desire to own two or three cars. For the plan to be meaningful, however, we need to establish benchmarks to determine whether you're meeting the objectives of your goals.

The goal can be less specific too. Perhaps you want your spendable income to grow by a certain percentage a year. You could just shoot for a big number in savings and investments, say, $1 million in ten years. The less specific or unachievable the target, though, the easier it will be to let it slide. How much money you want is an important question, one that we'll revisit throughout this book. It also leads to the question, Why do you want so much money?

This may sound like a silly question. You may not want *that* much more money, just a little bit more. How much is a little bit more? Twenty-nine-year-old Fred Reingold recently was forced to borrow $500 from a friend, and he makes $75,000 per year. Sounds absurd, doesn't it? Dave Bommer, a fellow who works in the printing business, earns $2,000 a month and has a small child to feed. Yet he recently purchased an $80,000 house.

On your initial visit to a financial planner he will ask about your plans and your financial goals. This is tantamount to saying "How much will you want and when?" At the risk of sounding platitudinous, you probably already make enough money to do most of what you want. The only question is timing. The real quandary is not how much, but how long you will have to wait to make your desire come true.

The second truism is that each increment to your earning power will always leave you wanting a little bit more. This may sound discouraging, especially from a book that promises to increase your spendable income. We can always dream up additional desires. Right now we probably have enough to do what we want. How much more do you need?

Your wants never run out. Your tastes grow right along with your ability to buy things. In fact, they outdistance them. You find that you no longer consider McDonald's when choosing where to eat. And your living space: You find that you just can't get by without a pool or a view or library or fireplace and so on. We resign ourselves to living within our means (or we should) as a matter of survival.

How We Treat Cash

How we treat money already in our pockets is a completely different story. In large part it is derived from the way our parents felt about money. If your parents treated money as a sacred resource, you probably have that same respect. Take Mary George. Her mother is a teacher, her father a preacher. Besides Mary, her parents had four other children to support. Obviously, excess money didn't float around in that household. Yet over the years her parents were able to establish a substantial nest egg. And Mary is the same way. Though she now earns $50,000 a year working for a Phoenix land-development firm and has over $150,000 in investments, she still spends her money frugally. And she saves conscientiously: 25 percent of her take-home pay.

Mary says, "My parents are very, very prudent. And they taught me the value of savings. After all, there wasn't a lot of cash around on which to raise five kids. I take home $3,000 per month, but I can live on about $1,000."

"Why do you want money and why are you so hell-bent-for-leather on getting it?" I ask.

"Security," she answers. "It's very important for me to know that I could live if I lost my job. It's so critical to have money. I don't live extravagantly."

I followed up. "How much money do you want?"

She was up front about her desires. "I still need to make a lot more. I'd like to go into my own business. So far, I've devoted my life to my career. It's time to start thinking about raising a family. And I suppose I'll do that soon. But since I'm making money, I don't necessarily need the security of a husband. That's why I think women of our generation aren't marrying as quickly. Today, we can make money. In the past it wasn't like that, and women had to get married as a form of security. Now having a family is becoming increasingly important to me. But I need to have that security."

Twenty-nine-year-old Janice Gordon is another case in point. She works for a retail firm in San Francisco and earns a healthy salary, in the low $30's. Recently she married a man of immense means. From his family's wealth alone, he has an individual net worth in the tens of millions. Despite her newfound freedom from financial constraints, she still scrimps, complains about spending two bucks on a beer, and cuts out discount coupons from the newspaper.

On the other hand, if your parents lived for the day, that, more than likely, is your attitude as well. I recognize the broadness of that generality, but the people I spoke with maintain that they have essentially the same outlook on money their parents had.

The relative amount of money people spend (or the percentage of their total income) has little to do with their overall income. Some people save a tremendous fraction of their incomes, while others couldn't save a nickel if their lives depended on it. The question remains: Why do you want money? During the research for this book I asked the people I spoke with this question and their responses seem to fall into four general categories.

What Money Does

First and most obviously, we want money so that we can buy things. Money enables us to provide for ourselves and others. At the most basic level, we need food and shelter and clothing.

Secondly, once past the basics, money offers creature comforts as well as a choice about how to spend time. For example, consider how you clean your clothes. If you're scrimping just to eat, you could wash your clothes in the sink. If you have some coins in your pocket, you wash your clothes in a coin-op machine, but that still requires going to the Laundromat. With a little more disposable income, you buy a machine so you don't waste your time sitting in a Laundromat. Further down the spectrum, you take your laundry out to be done or you have your live-in maid do it.

Each step represents a decision by you to trade off your time for additional expense. This type of choice reverberates far into our daily lives. You can take a bus to work. In many metropolitan areas in America, this can be a tortuous process. But if you can afford an alternative, you probably do. As you earn more money you can afford to drive according to your own schedule and pay gas, upkeep, and parking fees. Finally, as you pass into the arena of the truly wealthy, you get someone else to drive you to work as you sit in the back of your stretch limo, watch TV, talk on your cellular phone, and catch up on *The Wall Street Journal*. The choice is between spending time to save money and spending money to save time.

The third reason for desiring money is closely related. Provided we had a few leaves over our heads, our bodies could survive on beans, a little gruel, water, and a Gandhian weave. But our spending habits are also a function of what we want to say about ourselves. You can drive a BMW or you can drive a VW. Both cars do what they're intended to: provide transportation. When you buy a BMW, you make a statement to the rest of the auto-bound population and peers that says "I can afford a BMW." The same holds true for the Casio-watch wearers versus the Rolex crowd. Money offers the opportunity to make a statement about ourselves that we wish to convey to others. Your disposable income provides a scorecard in society of how well you're doing. There are many ways to earn respect and prestige, and money is only one. In America, however, making lots of money is still seen as a hallmark of glory and achievement.

Finally, money offers security. If some calamity should befall us or our families, we know we can support them during this time when the money tap is turned off. Indeed, the security-blanket reason for holding on to money and protecting it is the basis for one of the strongest human desires of obtaining money.

To sum up, money offers us four things: necessities, a choice of how to spend time, a benchmark of how well we're doing, and security. The point of this discourse is to raise some issues to help you think about how important making money is to you and why you want more.

I don't mean to be didactic or overly philosophical so early on. But you've got to look inside yourself to begin to understand which will be your best financial plan. To help you get a better grip on this question, I've got a few questions.

A Few Questions About Your Money Propensity

This test will help you to understand your own feelings toward money. I'll explain how at the end.

1. After you pay your rent or mortgage payment, your gas, electric, water, and telephone bills, your auto payments and insurance, your student loans, and any other commonly occurring expenses (except those over which you have direct control, such as health clubs and cable TV), how much money do you have left? Quick, if you know the answer without having to calculate it, mark "yes," otherwise, "no."
   YES_____   NO_____

2. How much money do you earn from your job annually?
   Less than $25,000 _____   Between $25,000 and $35,000
   _____   More than $35,000 _____

3. When you prepared your taxes last year did you use the long form *and* deduct expenses? ("Yes" for both, "no" otherwise.)
   YES_____   NO_____

4. Do you own your own residence or any other real estate that you yourself purchased? (Not that was willed or given to you.)
   YES_____   NO_____

5. Do you own any stocks, bonds, or mutual fund shares that you yourself bought?
   YES_____   NO_____

6. Have you ever dabbled in options?
   YES_____   NO_____

7. Do you have a stockbroker that you sought out?
   YES_____   NO_____

8. Have you ever owned precious metals as an investment, not as jewelry?
   YES_____   NO_____

9. Do you own any Certificates of Deposit (CD's)? If yes, when they come due, do you shop around for the best rate as opposed to letting them just roll over? (Mark "yes" for affirmations to both questions, otherwise "no.")
   YES_____   NO_____

10. Have you ever taken out a loan from a bank (excluding a car loan or credit cards)? (Real estate loans are acceptable.)
    YES_____   NO_____

11. For any loan ever taken out from a bank—even on credit cards—did you shop around for the best rate as opposed to simply going to the place where you had a checking account?
    YES_____   NO_____

12. Do you pay monthly checking-account charges?
    YES_____   NO_____

13. How is the Dow Jones Industrial Average doing? Do you know?
YES_____　NO_____

14. What is the current inflation rate? Do you know?
YES_____　NO_____

15. Do you read the business section of your newspaper regularly?
YES_____　NO_____

16. Do you read *The Wall Street Journal, Business Week, Fortune,* or *Forbes* regularly?
YES_____　NO_____

17. Do you have any outside sources of income, other than your job, from which you derive at least 10 percent of your annual income?
YES_____　NO_____

18. How much money do your parents have in the bank or in investments?
Less than $100,000 _____　Between $100,000 and $1 million _____　Greater than $1 million _____

19. For their retirement, have your parents planned beyond the company pension plan and social security benefits?
YES_____　NO_____

Here's how to score: Add up your "yes" answers. For those questions that had three possible responses, score 0 if you chose the first choice, 1 for the second, and 2 for the third. Add this number to the number of "yes" answers for your total score. I'll explain what your point tallies mean shortly.

My academic training is in economics. One precept of economic investigation and economic theory is that to understand people's actions, you watch what they do as opposed to listening to what they say.

The questions revolved around actions you have taken in the past. Not once did I ask something like "How much money *would* you like?" I didn't inquire about what you *would* like to do. I took your pulse about your past efforts at seeking out money. If you ranked high (+12), I categorize you as someone who expends a great deal of energy in trying to get ahead financially. You have chosen a career that pushes your cash flow right up there, you seek out stockbrokers who hold the promise of increasing your investment returns, you purchase real estate with an eye to capital gains, and you read up on the ways of finance and the business world.

If you scored between eight and twelve, you have an eye on your finances but it is not critical to you. You read the business section, you think about ways to make money but don't always follow through. You've begun to take hold of your financial picture.

Finally, if you're in the last category (less than 8), you have sought other things in life or you just may not have had the resources to seek out investments. Don't take umbrage if you find yourself in this last category. In the past you haven't devoted much attention to it. This is not to say that you can't make it in the future. Nor is it to say that you don't have the drive to obtain cash. All I'm saying, I repeat, is that you haven't sought out money in the past in a concerted fashion. Maybe you don't know how—indeed, that might have been the reason you bought this book in the first place.

I administered this questionnaire to the people you'll read about in this book. And without exception those people, who through their actions suggest that they will soon be well off, scored high. On the other hand, those people who didn't score as many points had not yet taken steps to improve their financial position.

An important point to remember: You won't make an extraordinary amount of money unless you really want to. You have to work at it.

This excursion into psychology has been to help you understand your attitude toward money a little better. This is the key to your financial success. Throughout this book I'll discuss a wide range of investment strategies and tactics. In the main, the investment framework for all young people is the same. Plan. Budget and save. Buy a home. Invest. And save some more. But it's the tactics for doing the steps that will differ according to your personality. That's why we explored this subject at the front of the book. Maybe you want to investigate individual stocks or maybe you would prefer to buy shares in a mutual fund. Maybe you'd like to search out rental property, fix it up, and rent it out. Or maybe that's too much effort and you'd rather just keep your money hard at work in a tax-free bond fund.

Despite the fact that I write about making money, I classify myself as belonging in the second category—those who are quasi-interested in making money. Except for an occasional foray into the stock market on an individual stock, I keep the bulk of my liquid assets in mutual funds. My long-term assets are in real estate. I enjoy writing and working at my career as opposed to minding the day-to-day fluctuations in my investment portfolio. I believe that this will earn a more than satisfactory return without the threat of a whupping. I am just not all that thrilled by the prospect of talking endlessly with stockbrokers and deciphering charts.

In sum, understand yourself and your disposition toward money by looking at the actions you have taken in the past. There is no guarantee of how to make the most money with the least amount of effort. The purpose of this book is to give you solid advice about what to do next. And I'll do that. We'll work out a plan for you. The plan's purpose is singular: to give you an approach, the perspective, you need to begin earning the greatest possible return on your available assets. But before turning to the plan, let's look at the central relationship in finance and the central concept to understand before you make any investments: risk and reward.

CHAPTER 3
The Risks and the Rewards

"Being smart" is one of the key tenets of our financial plan. Being smart requires an understanding of the general playing field of investments, of scams, of risks, and of rewards. In this short chapter we briefly touch on these issues to give you a flavor of risk and reward. Let's take a look at the experiences of Mary Morton and Sam Sorley. Mary's twenty-six and Sam's twenty-five. One or the other is likely to strike a familiar chord.

Ms. Morton strode into the elegant dining room of Boston's classy Locke-Ober restaurant to talk about the harrowing morning she had just put in for a predominant fund house. Propping her briefcase against the table, she settled in the finely upholstered chair. We had been classmates at Wharton together and had arranged this lunch to talk about life in the real world, our friends, and job opportunities.

As lunch arrived we spent a few minutes discussing how a company president had just that morning tried to convince Mary to write a glowing report about his company's latest high-tech mousetrap. "What's anybody going to do with a technology that allows you to open your garage door from anywhere in the world?" she asked, only half joking. The conversation quickly turned to money. Our own, that is, and we had plenty to say.

"I just don't understand it," Mary confided to me as she paid the tab with her American Express Card. "I'm pulling in more money than I ever have before. Yet, when payday rolls around, I don't seem to have anything left. And"—she lowered her voice— "I make $40,000 a year. Where's my money going?"

Good question, Mary. Now to Sam:

We sat in his Southern California stucco condo. It looked like it had been furnished by Budweiser and it contained, in fact, many hand-me-downs from his parents. Despite the general dilapidated state of the furniture, an elaborate state-of-the-art sound system and an expensive projection television were the central points of the living room. Strewn about on the orange crushed-velvet five-piece couch were various socks and orphan shoes. In short, the place had the look of a typical bachelor pad. Sam offered me a Bud as we began to talk.

"I got out of college about four years ago and went right to work for a major bank in California [Bank of America]. But, despite the fact that I was working for one of the world's largest financial institutions, I was making only $16,000 a year. From just recently being a student, living on next to nothing, that money sure seemed like a lot. Every two weeks they'd give me a check. I soon found out that I wasn't really making all that much. The problem was that I had this little piece of plastic, a credit card, that the bank gave me without question. I should have questioned it.

"Before things got out of hand, I tore up my credit cards and began to take stock of my financial situation. I still had pretty cheap rent and I started to think about buying a home. The problem was that in Los Angeles housing prices had just gone through the roof. It seemed to me that to buy a house would cost about the gross national product of several smaller nations. I knew, though, that this was what I wanted to do. I started to save my money. It was hard at first. All my friends, with their new credit cards, wanted me to go out all the time. I just knew that if I wanted to play that game, I'd never get ahead.

"After several years my salary had moved up to $20,000, I'd

accumulated several thousand dollars, and I made my move. I found a condo costing $50,000. Now, it wasn't the greatest place in the world. In fact, the neighborhood didn't seem like the kind of place that I'd ever envisioned moving to. When I looked around at housing prices in some of the nicer neighborhoods, though, I knew I was just fooling myself. So I bought the place with my savings and a loan of $1,500 for the down payment from my mother. It cut my taxes so I could save more money. Since then I've been making small investments in various mutual funds."

Which of these persons and their situation best describes you? Mary lets money control her while Sam has a good sense about money and what it can do for him. For many people money always seems to be too short—there's never enough. Our paychecks are big, but so are our expenses: the young professional's predicament.

By following my framework, you can improve your financial well-being. We'll get to where you control your finances, where you establish your investment returns, and where you set your financial destiny.

Alas, though, there is no one proven strategy (despite what many stockbrokers and financial planners will tell you). There are of course smarter ways to approach the subject, as well as dumber ones. In this chapter we'll focus on some investment scams and on risks and rewards. Clearly, as an intelligent investor, you'll have to understand an easy way to separate the worthwhile investments from the dross. Understanding risks and rewards will help you get a leg up on this important subject.

Mr. Ponzi

A friend comes to you and says that she has just made an investment that promises an 80 percent return per year. Do you invest? Unless inflation has reared its ugly head once again and bank money market funds are offering 25 percent, an 80 percent return on investment, or ROI, is unusually high and unusually suspect. There are two ways an 80 percent return can be earned and both risk your entire investment. The first is through leverage, which will be discussed at length later, and the second is by becoming an early investor in a Ponzi scheme.

The Ponzi scheme is named after Charles A. Ponzi, a swindler who became famous during the twenties. The scam is akin to a chain letter with evil intentions at its root. Initial investors are paid a fantastic return with the ringleader's money. At the second stage, after all the initial investors have told their friends about this great scheme—be it worm farms, shopping centers, second trust deeds, or racehorses—the money generated from the second round of investors is used to pay off the first set of investors. Cash from the third set of investors pays off the second set. Investors' funds are never invested in any asset; instead, the money just goes to the previous investors. And so on.

After a while the number of investors and the pool of money grow to a fantastic size. Sylvia Porter, who has turned financial planning into a cottage industry, notes that "the central factor in the inevitable collapse of a Ponzi scheme is that there really is no significant source of income—other than new, unsuspecting, naively greedy investors."* Finally, the ringleader says, "We're not getting enough new money coming in to pay the existing investors." The original investors grab the money, leave for the Bahamas, and the investors who joined last are left holding the bag.

No assets are seized because there never were any assets, despite the ringleader's claims about real estate, paper-laden forests, prolific and prodigious cows, solid-gold worm farms, or any of a multitude of things. The only asset was the expectations of more investors who'd heard about the good thing from earlier investors. And now there aren't enough new investors and there goes your money. The clear lesson: Beware of fantastic returns.

Riskandreturn

The state lottery, or Lotto, is another example of a worthless investment. When you fill out the little coupon and plunk down

---

* Sylvia Porter, *Sylvia Porter's New Money Book for the 80's* (New York: Avon, 1979), p. 670.

your money, you're making an investment in the broadest sense of the word. You're investing money with the hope of earning a sizable return. So do many others. The reason it's an unwise investment is that it's not a fair one. The states that run these contests do so for a purpose. When the state fathers raise money through the Lotto mechanism, they don't turn the entire pot of money that was wagered back to the gamblers. The extra money goes to fund the schools, senior citizens, or other worthy causes. In other words, the potential reward doesn't come anywhere near compensating you for the low likelihood that you'll win.

Any time you get close to the investment arena you hear the words *Risk and Return*. It's as if it were one word: *Riskandreturn*. There's a reason risk and return go hand in hand. You can always find the promise of a higher return. The trade-off, though, is that the higher the return, the less likely it is that your return will come through. Throughout this book and your investing life, keep this truism in mind: The more the return on an investment fluctuates, i.e., it has a low likelihood of occurrence, the higher the promised return from that investment should be. Conversely, if you see an extraordinarily high return on investment, the likelihood of achieving that high return is slim.

One million dollars is wagered on Lotto, yet the state plans on paying out only $500,000. If you were to play all the possible number combinations, you'd be assured of hitting the jackpot. It would cost you, though. You'd spend $1 million to generate an assured $500,000. You'd lose half your investment. In other words, for every dollar you bet, you can expect to lose 50 cents. Clearly, the game's returns aren't fair, making the lottery a poor investment choice.

In the next few paragraphs we'll analyze gambling games as investments. The intent is not to make you an expert in casino games. Instead, it is to give you an introduction to thinking about risk in an easy, systematic way. Risk, after all, is just the likelihood that a possible outcome will actually become a reality.

Casinos work on the same principle as Lotto, although the odds against winning aren't nearly as high. The people who run the casinos, however, are also in business to make money, so gamblers beware!

For instance, in roulette the payoff for hitting a selected number is 35 to 1. If you wager a $2.00 chip on a particular number and it hits, you win 35 chips. However, there are 35 numbers plus two other numbers: zero and double zero. These additional two numbers improve the house's odds. If you choose a number, say 7, the odds of hitting it are 37 to 1, not 35 to 1.

Again, as in the lottery scenario above, if you bet on all 37 spots, you're assured of hitting the right number. But it cost you 37 chips. The house, though, pays you only 35 chips for hitting the right number. The bottom line is that you lose two chips. It cost you $74 with $2.00 chips to earn $70. You automatically lose $4.00.

You can also bet on "Even" or "Odd" in roulette. The house pays one to one for this bet. You bet a chip on "Even," it comes up "Even," and you win an additional chip. Hence, by betting "Even" or "Odd," the chances of which are slightly worse than 2 to 1, your odds are greatly improved over selecting one number, but the payout is considerably lower. The risk is less—but so is the potential return (see Chart 2):

CHART 2

Risk and Return on Roulette

Bet	Return	Risk
1 on Even	1 to 1	17/37 or 46%
1 on Odd	1 to 1	18/37 or 49%
A Specific #	35 to 1	1/37 or 3%

What Game Are We Playing?

Gambling games nicely illustrate the central premise behind financial thinking: risk and return. With investments the risk cannot be seen nearly as neatly, and often those people who sell investments want to disguise the riskiness of their wares.

This premise holds that the greater the inherent risk in an investment product, the greater the return that product should promise, so that you will be induced to invest your money. Return simply means the amount of money you'll earn on your investment. If you put your money in a 5½ percent passbook savings account, your return is 5½ percent. Similarly, if you put $1,000 in a bank certificate of deposit (CD) for a year that promises an interest rate of 8 percent, your return will be 8 percent. There is no risk. You know what the return is going to be before you go into the venture.

"Risk" refers to how likely you are to see the promised return. The riskier investments could cause you to lose the entire amount that you put up in the first place. Less risky investments, while they won't steal away your initial investment, might not return what they say they will.

However, they might return even more than was first promised. The less risky investments are those that assure a given return, such as the bank CD's. The investments that offer a medium degree of risk are those for which the return might fluctuate, but the chances of a reduction in your original capital are slim. The highest-risk investments are those that assure neither return on nor preservation of investment capital (see Chart 3):

CHART 3

Potential Risk	Return
High Risk	Great Returns or Loss of Entire Investment
Medium Risk	Preservation of Capital Likely; Uncertain Rate of Return
Low Risk	Assured Preservation of Capital, Lowest Rate of Return

The maxim of risk and return is central to finance and to financial planning. As we investigate investment options I'll keep coming back to this point: That is, if you want to increase your potential return, you have to understand that you must increase the potential risk of your investment dollars. This principle holds true for all financial instruments. Bank money market funds, which are insured by the federal government, generally pay less than do uninsured money market mutual funds. And we'll see that stocks generally hold out the promise of a greater return—and greater risk—than the money market funds. Now that we've laid the groundwork by gaining an understanding of how money is made and lost and analyzing why you want money, let's build the foundation of your strategy: your plan.

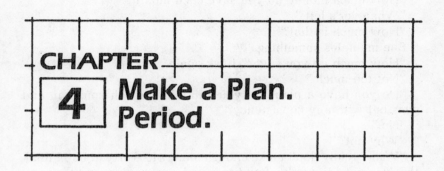

CHAPTER 4
Make a Plan.
Period.

Meredith Henderson is cheerful, perky, and sharp, and she has a certain joie de vivre that makes spending time with her a pleasure. She graduated from Vassar College and set her sights on the Big Apple. Today the twenty-seven-year-old lives in a fancy Upper West Side New York apartment, works for a design firm, and goes out on the town every weekend. Her life is grand and, financially speaking, she walks the fine line: she dines at restaurants frequently, dresses very well, and has a penchant for international travel. I asked her about money.

She says she really hasn't given it much constructive thought. I gave her the questionnaire testing money propensity and her responses suggest that, in fact, she has priorities other than accumulating wealth in her life. At least right now.

"How much money do you make, Meredith?" I asked.

"About $28,000," she said.

"What do you do with your money?"

"I pay rent—which is a lot, I pay my bills, my student loans, and buy groceries."

"Where does the rest go?"

"I don't know. Lamston's, I guess [a discount store with sundries and supplies]. Oh, and clothes and lunches. And, I guess I should include vacations."

"How much money do you save each month?"

"Whatever's left."

"How much is that?"

She mumbles something.

"How much do you save?" I ask again.

"Not too much."

"Do you have a plan? Do you know how much comes in and goes out with any consistency?"

"No."

"Why not?"

"Well, I really don't make enough money to worry about. I think that you need to work a few years and start saving, and then you can really do something."

"How much would you need to start to 'do something'?"

"I don't know."

Meredith earns a sufficient salary. She believes she's too young to have to worry about investing. She's able to meet her daily and monthly expenses, and she is comfortable. In fact, many with whom I've spoken echoed her sentiments on financial planning:

"I'm too young."

"I really don't make enough money."

"I will in a few years when I get _____." (Fill in the blank with "older," "more money," or "a better job.")

These are more excuses than explanations. I told her, as I'm about to explain to you, that you can make a financial plan and still enjoy life without having to screw your shoes to the floor. Just be smart and rational, and planning is incredibly simple. You don't have to make any decisions about where to place your hard-earned money (yet). You don't have to relegate your palate to spaghetti for dinner seven nights a week. You don't have to buy rental property and contend with tenant complaints. All you have to do is sit down with a pencil, a calculator, and some of the charts I'll provide you with in the coming pages. In the meantime, let's go through the intellectual steps necessary to create a plan that is workable for you.

Some Early Thoughts

When you use a map it's because you have a destination, an endpoint, but you don't know the best way to get there. It's the same with a financial plan. We need to determine a financial goal and we need a map to figure out the quickest and most direct way to reach that monetary destination. Simply put, a plan will help you get from here to there.

Moreover, it'll help you to understand the trade-offs you face. It will help you to minimize the big blows that inevitably occur and to use windfalls for productive purposes.

Is the following a sketch of your current financial picture? You manage to save a little money at the end of the month. Everything's going smoothly. Then the big blow(s). First, your car needs a major overhaul. Then vacation time rolls around, and you think you deserve a little vacation, so it's off to Tobago. Some time later on, an annual insurance bill shows up. You interview for a new job, so it's time to buy some new clothes. The list is long, and your savings just seem to dissipate. Every time you save up a little money, a large, somewhat unexpected expense knocks firmly on the front door and—puff!—there go the savings. You're back to square one. And, to make matters worse, that long-term goal of buying a house falls by the wayside.

That this list of unexpected expenses is long, that you can make such a list, and that these expenses do occur, not every month, but with painful regularity, means that you can plan for them. That's right, you can plan for unexpected expenses. A plan will help to alleviate these problems when they do occur.

Your Goals

If you don't own a house, that's your goal. I don't care how much money you make, or what tax bracket you're in, or what the size of your investment portfolio is, a house should be your goal. I touched on this briefly in the first chapter, but let's look further at why you need to own a house. (We'll undertake a full-blown examination in the real estate section.)

First, it satisfies the desire to have a home you can call your own. One long standing American dream is to own a place you can call your own. While the desire to own a home is not a financial explanation, there's a certain satisfaction that comes with saying "This is mine." Second, it offers some clear tax-saving advantages, and, finally, it is a sensible long-term investment. In survey after survey young people continue to claim that owning their own home is their goal. But they just don't know how to go about it in a financially astute way.

With regard to your house and the plan, you now need to know how much to save for your down payment and closing costs. You can determine this simply by finding out housing prices for your desired neighborhood. For this you'll have to check your local newspaper, chamber of commerce, or your local bank. This information is not hard to find.

Once you find the median housing prices for a small one-bedroom house or condo in your area, you can reduce that amount by an additional 10 percent. You're planning on buying a place at the low end of the price spectrum. The median sales price is just that —half the houses in your locale sold for more, while the other half sold for less than that. You're not moving into a mansion, so you should figure that your house will cost on the low side. (The low side of housing prices in your area, that is.)

You will need to make a down payment, which can vary from 5 percent to 25 percent of the total purchase price of your home. Mortgage banking has become a lot more competitive these days, and while many banks still require more than 20 percent down, there are some that will allow you to make a low down payment (5 percent or, more likely, 10 percent). You want to make as low a down payment as possible. Assume that closing costs, lawyers' fees, appraisal fees, title search, and whatever else the bank can think of will cost you another 5 percent. This amount, then, can be your target figure—5 percent to 10 percent for the down payment and 5 percent for closing costs, or a total of 10 percent to 15 percent of the estimated purchase price for houses in your area.

I've included a list of median housing prices throughout the country as of June 1986 (Chart 4). Housing inflation rates vary, so this information is invariably out of date. You just need an approximation at this stage.

CHART 4

Median Housing Prices for Major Metropolitan Areas

Metro Area	Price	Estimated Cash Required to Move In*
Atlanta	$ 86,400	$10,137
Boston	$159,000	$20,711
Chicago	$ 86,000	$13,500
Dallas	$ 76,000	$12,015
Los Angeles	$150,300	$33,018
New York City	$189,000	$47,185
Phoenix	$ 80,500	$ 8,401
Seattle	$ 83,100	$13,230

* Typical prices for 1,400 to 1,600 square feet with three bedrooms, two baths, living room-dining room area, two-car garage, close to schools and shopping centers. All mortgages have fixed 15- or 30-year terms. Cash to Move In includes down payment and closing costs.

Source: "Home: Price Split Boston Bananas, New York Nuts," *Money* (New York City: Time, Inc., August 1986), p. 34.

If you already own a home, we need to establish another goal. If you have children, how many years before they go to college? Average four-year private education costs are hovering around $40,000 at this writing. You can use the chart below, which assumes a 6 percent per year increase* in education costs, to deter-

* "Annual Cost of College Will Rise 6 Percent This Fall," *The New York Times*, August 4, 1986, p. A9.

mine how much money you'll need by the time your youngsters sign up for freshman classes. This goal may seem like a faraway one, but the earlier you begin, the easier it will be. Furthermore, starting early expands the range of investment options available to you as you strive toward your goal. Because you can invest in riskier assets, given your longer-term perspective, you may find yourself in an even better position than you'd originally planned (see Chart 5):

CHART 5

How Much You'll Need When Your Child Is Old Enough for College

(Assumes $40,000 for Four Years, 6% Increase per Year)

Child's Age	Years to Go	$'s Needed
18	0	$40,000
17	1	$42,000
16	2	$44,000
15	3	$46,305
14	4	$48,620
13	5	$51,051
12	6	$53,604
11	7	$56,284
10	8	$59,098
9	9	$62,053
8	10	$68,414
7	11	$71,834
6	12	$75,426
5	13	$79,197
4	14	$83,157
3	15	$87,315
2	16	$91,681
1	17	$96,265
0	18	$101,078

You don't have kids, and you already own a house. What should you shoot for? How about your parents? Do you want to start socking away a little money for your parents' golden years? You can use the same methodology you used for the kids in college to determine how much money you'll need and when. In X number of years you want to provide them with Y number of dollars each year. How much do they earn now? How much will they need to live in the same style later? Will their house be paid up? From their current monthly income, subtract social security benefits and planned benefits from the pension plans in which they're currently enrolled. The net figure is how much you'll need, per year, to provide for them when they reach sixty-five (see Chart 6):

CHART 6

Helping Out Your Folks

Their Current Monthly Income	_____
Less Monthly Social Security Benefits	_____
Less Monthly Pension Benefits	_____
= Total Amount Needed per Month	_____
× 12 = Yearly Amount	_____

Of course if they've been saving and investing all their lives, you may not need to provide any support. Most people, however, typically rely on social security and their pension-plan benefits to fund their older years. And, as you'll recall from the inflationary late 1970s, many people found themselves in terribly unfortunate situations. Who's to say that we won't experience another such situation between now and the time our parents retire?

Zero Coupon Bonds and Your Future

Goals such as these—kids in college and the parents' later years—require you to come up with a predetermined sum in a known number of years. A relatively recent financial innovation called the zero-coupon bond may be your answer. Some investment houses have given their zero-coupon bonds (or simply "Zeros") feline-sounding acronyms such as TIGERs and CATS, for questionable marketing reasons. These products provide you with a predetermined amount that comes due in a specified number of years. To understand why Zeros are unique investment products, we need to consider the traditional bond. (And they are *products*. You buy them and they provide benefits, just like a car, a TV set, or a house. Never forget this when you're investing your money— you're buying something and you need to scrutinize it, just like any other high-priced item you'd buy.)

A bond is a loan. It's a loan that you make to a company or a government unit which it then uses to finance its operations. In most cases you receive a payment twice a year. This payment is called a coupon, stemming from the old days when you received a coupon book along with the bond. Actual coupons were re-deemed (cashed in) for payment every six months. The coupon rate is the interest rate the originating company or government unit agrees to pay annually. For instance, say the South Eastern Pennsylvania Transit Authority (SEPTA) wants to borrow $350 million to buy new buses. The Authority goes to the investment community and offers to pay a market rate, say 7 percent, for twenty-year bonds.

If the individual note has a face value of $1,000, that means you pay or invest $1,000 up front. They pay you $70 per year (really $35 twice a year), or 7 percent, and in twenty years they give you back your initial $1,000.

Zero-coupon bonds are similar except, as the name implies, there are no coupons to cash in for your semiannual interest pay-ments. In fact, there are no semiannual interest payments.

"What kind of deal is that?" you say. "I pay $1,000 today and twenty years from now they give me my $1,000 back?" Not ex-actly. These bonds are sold at a deep discount, which, in nontech-nical terms, simply means that you don't pay as much for these bonds up front.

When the sellers of these bonds decide how much to charge for them, they use the prevailing market interest rate (7 percent in our example) and figure out the price today, which, when com-pounded at 7 percent annually over twenty years, will equal

$1,000. In our SEPTA example, if the face value of the bond was $1,000 and the rate was 7 percent, and if they were zero-coupon bonds, you'd pay only $258 today to acquire one. Similarly, if you bought the bond for $258 today, that means in a year's time, if interest rates remain constant, its value would be $276:

Price Today	+	7% Interest	=	Price Next Year
$258	+	$18	=	$276

By similar reasoning, at the end of the second year your investment would be worth $298.86. At the end of the nineteenth year your investment would be worth $934.58. This amount, when compounded at 7 percent, will finally equal $1,000 as the twentieth year comes to a close. This chart simplifies matters (see Chart 7).

This example highlights how a little planning and foresight today will lead you to exactly where you want to be in a specified time period in the future, e.g., if you need $1,000 in twenty years, you can plan for that cost today. A corollary from the above example is that you can fulfill a future obligation today at a fraction of the cost.

It's cheaper. That's right. This is why planning is critical to financial success. Today I know that sometime in the next five years something will go wrong with my car that will more than likely cost $1,000 to repair. When that happens it'll cost one thousand bucks. Pure and simple. But had I had the foresight to know this five years ago (which is not altogether unreasonable) and the motivation to act on this information, I could have bought a zero-coupon bond yielding 7 percent for only $705 today:

Time	Value
1988	$705
1989	$756
1990	$811
1991	$869
1992	$923
1993	$1,000

CHART 7

Year	Beginning Investment Value	+	Year's Return at 7%	=	End of Year Investment Value
1	$258.42		$18.09		$276.51
2	$276.51		$19.36		$295.86
3	$295.86		$20.71		$316.57
4	$316.57		$22.16		$338.73
5	$338.73		$23.71		$362.44
6	$362.44		$25.37		$387.82
7	$387.82		$27.15		$414.96
8	$414.96		$29.05		$444.01
9	$444.01		$31.08		$475.09
10	$475.09		$33.26		$508.35
11	$508.35		$35.58		$543.93
12	$543.93		$38.08		$582.01
13	$582.01		$40.74		$622.75
14	$622.75		$43.59		$666.34
15	$666.34		$46.64		$712.99
16	$712.99		$49.91		$762.90
17	$762.90		$53.40		$816.30
18	$816.30		$57.14		$873.44
19	$873.44		$61.14		$934.58
20	$934.58		$65.42		$1,000.00

Your Own Business

How about running your own business? It's a dream that ranks right up there in the collective American paradigm, along with owning your own house. Many people seem to have a goal of running their own business. Probably only 5 percent will ever try. And of that 5 percent only half will succeed. These aren't great odds, yet you may have this strong urge to strike out on your own.

To go into your own business requires truckloads of money—

more money than you can possibly imagine. Most of it won't be your own if you're good at fund-raising and can impress bankers. Nevertheless, you need seed money. You've got to put up some of your own. Set $20,000 as your goal. It probably won't be enough, but as you home in on your idea several years from now, you'll start to get a clearer and clearer notion of how much you need. You can fortify your plan later to come up with additional money. (Sure, legends float around about people who, with no more than the clothes on their back, were able to establish multimillion-dollar enterprises. I would argue that cases like this are few and far between. The vast majority of start-up businesses fail precisely because managers underestimate the amount of capital the venture will need before the revenues come cascading in.)

You don't have any kids, your parents are already taken care of, you already own your own house, and you're happy with your job. Now what do you plan for? To make more money for money's sake? Exactly. For you we need to establish more esoteric goals. As a consequence your goal may simply be to enjoy a more afflu-ent life-style. Your basic objective could be to increase your after-tax earnings by 15 percent to 25 percent each year. At that rate you'll double the amount of money you have at your disposal in three to five years. A related goal is to earn enough money from your investment returns to cover your basic living expenses in ten years. You could quit your job and retire at the ripe old age of thirty-five.

Where You Are Now

Every financial planning guide I have ever read usually com-mences by undertaking what's called *The Personal Financial In-ventory* or *Your Financial Position* or *Statement of Personal Fi-nancial Well-being*. Replete with these heavy-sounding names comes a request for a DETERMINATION OF YOUR FINANCIAL POSITION. "You're just like a corporation," these authors hypoth-esize, "so you should treat your financial affairs just like one."

Well, you're not a corporation. You don't get paid for doing the financial rundown on your own position. Most likely you're not an accountant. These things tend to be academic. You go through the steps, you get out your calculator and your green eyeshades, your tax forms from years gone by, your statements from the mutual funds, your stock certificates, your deeds—all of 'em—and then you come up with YOUR NET WORTH. Your net worth doesn't matter a whit to anyone, save your mother and you—for your own financial aggrandizement. What is important is your liquid net worth, the money you have at your fingertips to invest.

In calculating financial self-worth, some say, "Make an inventory of your possessions to determine your assets." To that, again, I say, "Nuts." You're not a corporation about to undergo liquidation proceedings. You would never go out and sell your TV set. The same holds true for so-called collectibles. If you acquire antiques as an investment, fine, then include them in your financial picture. If, on the other hand, you collect antiques because you like to have them around the house, there's really no point in considering them when determining your net worth. You wouldn't sell these items, so why include them? We're about to go through an exercise to determine your *available* net worth. This is the crucial figure in your course of financial planning.

My aim is to make you financially sharp. Having achieved this, you'll be able to sort out decisions regarding money. In the future you'll invariably be faced with new financial instruments that aren't even around as I write this. My intent in these exercises is not to see how well you can figure them out, or how precise you can be with the decimal points, but to provide you with the vehicles to determine your present financial status and aspirations and to make you understand how you can reach those goals.

With that in mind, you're about to set off on a journey to establish *Your Available Personal Financial Wealth Inventory.* Rest assured, though, that it won't be nearly as arduous as it could be. Please fill out the "Where You Are Now" work sheet. Do it now (see Chart 8).

CHART 8

The "Where You Are Now" Work Sheet

Assets

Checking Account Balance . . . . $_____

Savings Account Balance . . . . $_____

Mutual Fund Balance . . . . $_____

Stock Portfolio . . . . $_____

Money Market Fund Balances . . . . $_____

Other Account Balances . . . . $_____

Equity in Your House . . . . $_____
(only if it exceeds 20% of the market
    value)

Other Investments/Assets . . . . $_____
(but not your car or household luxuries or
    goods or your IRA)

   Total Assets Owned . . . . $_____

Liabilities

Short-Term (those that will be paid within
    five years) Owed on:

   Credit Cards . . . . $_____

   Bank Loans . . . . $_____

   Loan from Parents (if payable within
       five years) . . . . $_____

   Any Loans You Can Pay Off within 5
       Years . . . . $_____

   Your Car . . . . $_____

   Student Loans (within the next 5
       years) . . . . $_____

Longer-Term

   Student Loans . . . . $_____

   Other Loans You Can't Get Out of in a
       Hurry . . . . $_____

   Total Liabilities Owed . . . . $_____

Net Worth (total owned less total owed) $_____

There it is. Your available net worth. If you skipped over this little exercise, please fill it in now. It really shouldn't take long, and it will make the rest of the book that much more worthwhile.

We now have an idea where you stand today. I haven't taken into account any moneys you really don't have at your disposal. For instance, I haven't included your house or condo. Its value as an asset is great, but cost as a liability is probably almost as great. And unless you plan to sell it *and* pocket the gain (a tough trick because you have to live somewhere), you really can't count that in your financial position. (If you own more than 20 percent of its market value, you may be able to borrow against it. In that case, it does represent an asset you can leverage.) Similarly, I have not included assets that are not primarily investment assets —for example, your car. While you may have paid much money for it, after taking repairs and maintenance into account, you shouldn't count on being able to sell it for a gain.

The last step in the program is to determine your financial life horizon. That's a heady name for a simple step that says "Here's where I am today, and here's where I want to be next year, the following year, and the years after that."

Your Financial Life Horizon

Determining where you want to go is a tough job. Look at your life over the past several years. It's changed a lot. When you were in college you probably couldn't have foreseen what you're doing now. Take the case of twenty-eight-year-old Chip Ketchrum. Chip thought he wanted to be a college professor in economics. He was smart, close to brilliant, and he liked the logical reasoning that constituted economics. As time went on Chip discovered that he was good at convincing people that he understood the business economics, that is, the financial management of, businesses. To-day, just four years after completing graduate school, Chip finds himself married to Meryl, an Italian woman, living in Rome, and jetting all over Europe convincing managers to change their business organizations. He's an international management consultant.

Certainly his life has taken twists and turns that he could never have predicted four years ago. He has, however, followed a wise path with his personal finances. First, he's a member of the $1,000-a-month club, that is, he saves $1,000 a month, which amounts to 20 percent of his gross monthly income. That's for starters. The total amount saved isn't as important as the percentage saved. Sure he makes a hefty chunk of change. But, in a 42 percent tax bracket, he also pays a hefty chunk in taxes. He has his savings/investments in municipal zero-coupon bonds because when he gets back to the States in three years, he wants to be able to afford a substantial down payment on a house. The remainder of his liquid assets are in a money market fund and in a high-growth mutual fund. Chip *could* be a little more adventurous with his investments, but his risk tolerance is low. When I asked him to fill out the Propensity to Money questionnaire, he scored high. He's interested in money, all right, but he doesn't want to make too many risky investments.

Even though his life has changed in ways he could never have imagined only a short while ago, Chip has accurately and succinctly planned his financial path. Life is a series of options: how we choose to spend our time; what we do to earn a living; what school to attend; where we live; the intensity with which we attack our work and our leisure activities. The world is our oyster, and so on and so forth.

Our financial lives can be construed in much the same manner. As I argued earlier, we have all made choices in the past about how much effort we expend in pursuit of the buck. Now let's look at the flip side: When we get those bucks, where do they go?

You have at the base level one financial choice: Spend now or save now and spend later. Currently you probably earn money through your job and possibly a token amount through your investment returns. At the midpoint of your life a greater and greater percentage of your income will be derived from investment returns. Finally, at the sunset of your life, all your income will come from investment returns (see Chart 9). If your only investments are a pension plan from work and your social security payments, these investments—and they are investments—will pay out a shallow return.

There are some people, unfortunately probably most people, who continue to earn the bulk of their income through their salary throughout their lives. You don't want to be one of these people. The purpose behind financial planning is to earn a greater and greater amount of your income through investment returns. This is how the majority of people we would consider financially successful have done it.

We spend money on groceries, on rent, on going out to eat, on movies, on bus fare, on automobile repairs, on utilities, and so on. Most, if not all, items in your discretionary expense column is "spending," not "saving."

We save money in money market funds, bank savings accounts, mutual funds, and in the principal portion of the monthly mortgage payments. Saving to me connotes more than just a passbook savings account. It literally means anything that (1) is not spending and (2) promises to generate a return. One way of differentiating among the various savings and investment products is through the rate of return promised by the brokers or sales brochures, e.g., Ginnie Mae funds at 10 percent, money market funds at 5¾ percent, and so on.

You'll note that I always refer to saving as "saving and investing." Indeed, we can save by putting money in a mattress. This, however, is not investing. Any other method of saving money that promises a return is, in fact, investing. And you should view it this way. You're not just saving money for a rainy day—you're saving money so that you can invest it.

Why save money instead of spending it? That's a universal question that can be answered in myriad ways. There are two reasons to save today: You get gratification from having saved the money, and you can almost always spend more tomorrow than you can today. As you grow older your fixed expenses will also grow. In ten or twenty years you can add in the kids' college expenses as a fixed expense. Almost invariably you'll be living in plusher surroundings. Your Mercedes will cost a whole lot more than the Nissan you have today. Everything will cost more.

A few pages back we looked at how zero-coupon bonds could be inexpensively bought today to pay for your parents' retirement

CHART 9

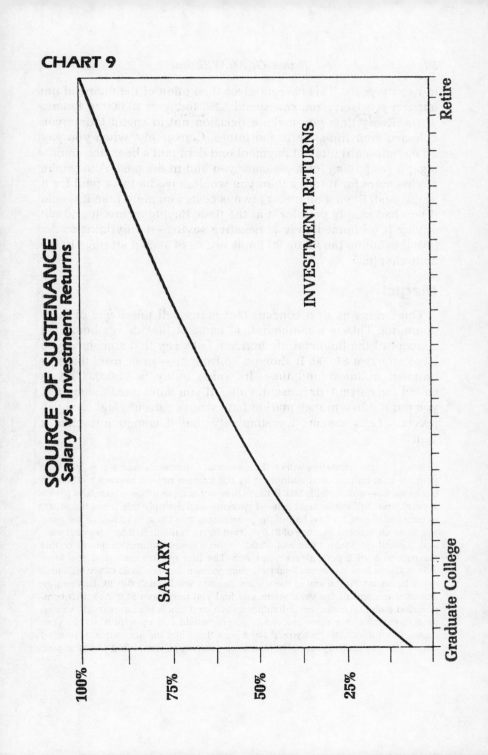

SOURCE OF SUSTENANCE
Salary vs. Investment Returns

in twenty years. This characterizes the notion of the financial life horizon precisely. You can spend $250 today or $1,000 in twenty years. Every time you make a decision not to spend today, you enhance your life-style in the future. Conversely, when you pay off a credit-card interest payment and debt that's been accumulating, you're paying for a pleasure you had in the past. And you're paying more for it today than you would have had you paid for it in the past. Buying on credit always costs you more than it would if you had simply paid for it at the time. Buying on credit and not paying it off immediately is negative saving—a silly thing to do. (We'll examine the financial implications of such a strategy in the next chapter.)

Magic!

This brings us to a concept that many call the magic of compounding. This is a mathematical concept that drives home the concept of the financial life horizon. Let's say that somehow you have an extra $1,000. It showed up from heaven or from the government at tax-refund time. Its value today is $1,000. This is called the current, or present, value. If you don't need the money, you put it into a money market fund whose current yield is, say, 8 percent. Let's assume for simplicity that it compounds once a year.*

* Here's how compounding works. If the account compounds once a year, you take your account balance and multiply it by the interest rate—8 percent × $1,000 in our example—which yields $80. If the instrument compounds semiannually (twice a year), take half the interest rate—4 percent—and multiply this times the $1,000 to earn $40 during the first half of the year. Going into the second half of the year, you have an account balance of $1,040. That figure is multiplied by 4 percent also, and you end up at year's end with $1,082. If the account compounds quarterly, this means you earn 2 percent every quarter. The first quarter ends and you have $1,020. Going into the second quarter, your account balance is $1,020, which also earns 2 percent. At the end of the second quarter, you have $1,040.40. This continues until the end of the year, when you find you now have $1,082.40. If it compounded daily, take 8 percent, divide it by 365, and this is the interest rate earned each day. Using this same methodology, you would end up with $1,083 in your account, not the $1,080 that would have been there had the account compounded once a year. After ten years of compounding daily, you would find $2,225 in your

At the end of the year you'll have $1,080 in that account. Instead of spending that $1,000 today, you could invest it and have $1,080 at the end of the year. At the end of the second year, you again face that choice: Spend or save. You've done fine without it for the first year, so you go for it once more. You again earn 8 percent. At the end of the second year, you find yourself with an account balance of $1,166 ($1,080 × 8% + $1,080 = $1,166). Again, you face that choice, and so on. After ten years of making the savings choice, the correct one, your investment would be worth $2,159, a gain of 215.9 percent (see Chart 10):

CHART 10

Year	Initial Investment	Previous Periods' Interest	Interest on Initial Investment	Interest on Interest	Total Investment
1	$1,000	$ 0	$80	$ 0	$1,080
2	$1,000	$ 80	$80	$ 6	$1,166
3	$1,000	$166	$80	$13	$1,260
4	$1,000	$260	$80	$21	$1,360
5	$1,000	$360	$80	$29	$1,469
6	$1,000	$469	$80	$38	$1,587
7	$1,000	$587	$80	$47	$1,714
8	$1,000	$714	$80	$57	$1,851
9	$1,000	$851	$80	$68	$1,999
10	$1,000	$999	$80	$80	$2,159

At an 8 percent interest rate, it is said that the value in the future, ergo, the future value, of your $1,000 investment in the money market fund will be $2,159. Consider it as follows: that $1,000 is the present value of $2,159 in ten years. This may sound

---

account—3 percent, or $66, more than if it compounded annually. You say "Big deal, a 3 percent difference." By doing a little more legwork up front, you can increase your return. Over the ten years you don't have to do continual checking; you've set your investment on automatic to earn as high a return as possible in this particular investment category.

like doublespeak. It does have some import, however, in charting your financial plan.

The magic of compounding is something I've been alluding to all along. It simply refers to the fact that every year, if you reinvest the prior year's gain, your investment starts from a higher base than the year before. You earn 8 percent on $1,000 in the first year. The second year, if you allow your investment return of $80 to remain in the same account, you begin the year with $1,080.

This example has a common theme: a choice, a trade-off between spending today and saving today and spending an even greater amount tomorrow. This is the financial life horizon. Over the hills and valleys of your upcoming life, you'll have many opportunities to save and invest your money. You'll have an even greater opportunity to spend that money. The trade-off reflects your choice, your action in your financial life horizon. If you want a big hill of beans in ten years, that means you'll have to do without a modicum of beans today. If you want a house to call your own in three years, you'll have to live more Spartanly than you would if you thought tomorrow was the last day of your life. If you want your kids to go to college, you'll have to start putting something away today (i.e., doing without something today). And your parents' golden years . . . Are the tears welling up yet?

This may seem like a big push toward guilt and deprivation. Don't take it that way. We can arrange your affairs today (which we'll do in the next chapter) to reduce your expenses as much as possible without dampening your life-style. But once this is done you need to get out the scalpel and do some financial reconstructive surgery. Further, another concept I'll introduce in the next chapter is that saving can have its own value. That is, you might just gain more satisfaction from saving your funds instead of going out for dinner for the fourth night this week.

The finishing touches to the skeleton of the financial program we're laying out for you is the "Financial Life Horizon" work sheet. In this we try to determine just how much money you'll need to do what it is you say you want to do. The aim of this exercise is to figure out how much money you need today to achieve your goal. First, we determine the present value of your goal—that is, how much you would need today to achieve your goal in however many years you specified earlier. Second, we subtract your current net available assets. What's left is how much you need to save and earn from your investments. Get out a pencil and fill in this next work sheet (see Chart 11).

CHART 11

GOALS

The "What Do I (We) Want and When" Work Sheet

Goal	Cost	Number of Years
A House	_____	_____
College for the Kids	_____	_____
Money for Parents	_____	_____
Increase Earnings 15% Per Year*	_____	5 Years
(Double current take-home pay)		
Your Own Business	$20,000	5 Years
Real Estate Investment	$10,000	5 Years
Other	_____	_____
(Use round numbers)		

* Increasing your salary at 15% per year will double your salary in five years. Simply double your salary for this choice.

At this early stage you should fill in only one goal. If you don't own a house, that should be the priority. Now we have an idea of where you want to go. Even if this doesn't describe your desires perfectly, you should fill in something as it will make the next section more relevant.

To get from here to there, fill in this:

Net available assets (from earlier chart)_____

Now we know where you are today and where you want to get to tomorrow. The final step is determining how long it will take you to achieve your goal, given the current interest-rate environment.

The Years-Rates Chart:
The Present Value of $1,000

Years		1	2	3	4	5
Rates	5%	$952	$907	$864	$823	$784
	6%	$943	$890	$840	$792	$747
	7%	$935	$873	$816	$763	$713
	8%	$926	$857	$794	$735	$681
	9%	$917	$842	$772	$708	$650
	10%	$909	$826	$751	$683	$621

This table is calculated to show how long it will take to save $1,000 at various interest rates. That is, it indicates that you'll need X dollars today to have $1,000 in your pocket in a given number of years, taking current interest rates into consideration. For example, let's say you need $1,000 in five years to fix your car and interest rates stand at 6 percent today. By looking at the intersection of five years and 6 percent you learn that you'd need to have $747 in the bank today to achieve that goal.

The exact steps follow:
1. To use these tables effectively, you need to determine the current rate on one-year bank CD's. (Bank certificates of deposit fluctuate with the market and frequently are around the lowest rates you could expect to earn on your money. Simply look in the business section of today's newspaper and you'll find advertisements by banks stating the current offering rate. Even if you find differing rates, estimate an average and round off the number. With this information, find the appropriate column and row.)
2. Divide the dollar amount you need in the future by $1,000. Multiply the factor circled in the Years-Rates Chart.
3. Subtract the difference between what you need today and (calculated in step 2) from what you already have as your net available assets listed above.

4. This is how much you'll need in your savings and investment account before you can reach your goal.

An example will make this clearer. Let's say interest rates are 6 percent and you would like to have an asset base of $12,000 within three years to make the down payment and cover closing costs on a house. From your net available assets information, we know you have $8,000 at your disposal. In other words, you'll need $4,000 in three years.

We take $4,000 and divide by $1,000 to get a factor of 4. The Years-Rates Chart tells us the present value for that combination is $840. We multiply this by 4 to arrive at $3,358. That's the amount you would need to save to reach your goal within three years.

This is a simplified form of your financial life horizon. You know what you want and you know how long you have to get there. We based the rates on bank CD's because they are among the safest financial instruments around. If you save and invest your money in such a fashion, you are guaranteed to hit your target. But if you don't have enough today, there are two ways to achieve your target: You can increase your net available assets, or you can seek a higher rate of return. The rest of the book is devoted to these two topics.

I realize this has been some tough sledding. Don't give up. In the upcoming chapters I will introduce stories of people who have achieved their targets by both increasing their nest egg and enhancing their rate of return. Further, we'll examine in depth how you can build your asset base and earn a higher return. Plow ahead.

SECTION

B BUDGET

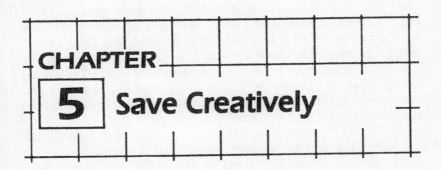

CHAPTER 5 Save Creatively

Bill Johnson complains incessantly about money. He never has enough. Keep in mind, though, that twenty-five-year-old Bill has no wife, no kids, no car, no cats, and only one frail dog to support. And Bill makes $36,000—that's $693 each week.

For the vast majority of Americans, that's enough money. But for Bill it's not. "If I just made a little more money, I'd be able to . . ." is his battle cry. Alas, money controls Bill's life. This isn't to say that he doesn't go out a lot. This isn't to say that he doesn't dress well, and hasn't seen the latest movies. This is to say, however, that Bill doesn't have firm control over his financial life horizon. He lives from paycheck to paycheck. Credit cards are a way of life for him—saving and investing are things that only people who are far richer than he can afford to do.

In the other corner we have Doug Heford. He worked as an auditor for IBM for nine years. During that time he amassed a stock portfolio currently valued at $60,000. There are only three ways he could have accomplished such a feat. First, he could have been given the money. He wasn't. Second, he could have invested $1,000 in options and made a killing overnight. He didn't. Third, he could have saved money, made his first stock investment for $3,000, continued to save and invest money in New York Stock Exchange stocks, and parlayed any gains into further investments. And that's what he did. When he began investing in individual stocks he was making $22,000 a year. Doug says, "I enjoy making money, and I know that making money requires saving and investing. I like doing that." Unlike Bill, Doug knows what it takes and he does it.

If your saving and investing habits are more like Bill's than Doug's, then this chapter will help you to establish a saving and investing regimen. Even if you have tight control over your spending, you will still pick up some tips.

Bill "saves" whatever he has left at the end of the month. It's not surprising that this amount, more often than not, is zero. He hasn't said to himself, "I want to save $100 this month. That means I won't be able to buy a new _____." If he decided that he was going to save and acted accordingly, at the end of the month he would have that $100 in his saving and investment account. This in and of itself would be a source of satisfaction.

At the beginning it will require considerable willpower. Over time it will just be a part of your life-style, like doing the laundry or buying groceries. There's no law saying that you have to spend everything you earn. We condition ourselves, though, to look in our checkbooks and say, "Whew, I've still got $150 to last me until the end of the month." Not surprisingly, by the month's end you've found new and creative ways to spend that remaining money. Back to square one.

Shotgun Approach

In this chapter we're going to point a shotgun at your expenses and spending habits. First, we're going to scout out just where you're spending your money. Then, we're going to aim at the superfluous expenses. Finally, we're going to take a cold, hard, calculated look at some of your spending. The net result is that you'll know exactly how you spend your money. I hope to change the way you think about the whole issue of spending money. It will require a shift in the way you view your money and its relationship to you. It's what I call a shift in paradigm. We'll discuss this concept at the conclusion of the chapter.

As you begin to save up a little bit you'll find that something else happens. It's somewhat of a paradox: You begin to feel more relaxed about spending money. The Bills of the world feel ever so guilty about spending money. "I'm spending too much," he says as he hands over his credit card at Brooks Brothers. You needn't feel guilty about spending money. The only way not to feel guilty, besides simply avoiding the issue, is to gain a firmer, surer hand on your financial picture.

How much do you save each month? It should be at least 10 percent of your gross monthly income. If not, that's the number to shoot for. If you do not save at least $100 a month at this time, make that your goal. But there's nothing wrong with saving only $50 a month. If you don't save even that much, set it as your target.

Many people, as they go through this exercise, say to themselves, "I've really got to save a big chunk. Otherwise, it won't really amount to anything." Nonsense. It's a little bit like saying "I want to go into business and I need a million dollars to start." Chances are you're never going to go into business because you'll never have that first million. You have to start small. Remember, if you're saving zero now, $50 per month is a significant increase.

However, if you begin saving too large an amount as compared with your current savings from, say, $50 to $500 a month, your efforts might be self-defeating. During that first month you'll show real drive and determination. You'll stock up on a six-month supply of beans; your cabinets will overflow with spaghetti. At the end of the second week you'll pitch your fork into the beans with despair and say, "If this is what saving money is all about, I don't want it. I don't care if I die in the poorhouse."

You've set your sights too high. You can't achieve your goal at this early stage, you'll give up, and you'll find yourself back at the starting line. There's nothing wrong with starting at a low figure, if necessary. As I've shown in some of the earlier examples, making money isn't something that's going to happen overnight. You've got to plan, you've got to be patient, and you must realize that these things take time. Let's look at some superstar savers.

The $1,000-a-Month Club

The $1,000-a-Month Club. Only a select few can join in. I'm not talking about a Christmas Club. Nor am I talking about a club where they *give* you $1,000 twelve times a year. It's the select group who can literally save $1,000 per month.

If you make less than $1,000 a month from your salary, you can't join the $1,000-a-Month Club. You'd be surprised, though, how many people who actually take home three and four times that amount can't save $1,000 a month. Or even $500. Or even $100.

Consider these differing experiences. Dave Lewis, thirty, earns $42,000 per year as a security analyst for a major mutual fund. His take-home pay amounts to $30,000, of which he saves $12,000, or 40 percent, of his take-home pay. Sally Randall, industrial engineer, twenty-eight, earns $52,000 per year, takes home $38,000, and saves $12,000, or 31 percent, of her take-home pay each year. Brenda Heathrow, who sells business forms, earns $32,000 per year, takes home $25,000, and saves $1,200, or 5 percent, of her take-home pay.

And then there's Linda McDonald, management consultant, twenty-nine years old, who earns $65,000 per year, takes home $45,000, and saves zip. . . . What? . . . Juanita Helms, investment banker, age thirty-one, earns $60,000 per year, takes home $45,000, and she, too, saves nothing. Roger Becker, reporter, earns $24,000 per year, takes home $18,000, and saves $7,200, or 40 percent, of his take-home rewards.

It almost seems as if how much money you save has nothing to do with how much money you earn. Certainly at low-income levels, where you're forced to dig for seeds for nourishment and pull a piece of cardboard over your head for shelter, saving money is just a passing thought. Once you earn more than the minimum required for getting by day to day, you decide how much to spend and how much to save. This is demonstrated by my examples above, where the percentage of take-home salary saved and invested ran the gamut. And this is a critically important point. How much money you save is a function of how much you don't spend. It sounds silly and self-evident. It seems like something everyone should know. And it's probably something everyone does understand, but most choose to ignore.

In completing research for this book, I read many financial planning books and found that saving, as a subject, is largely ignored. It is understandable yet inexcusable. Saving is boring; it doesn't make your blood race; you can't swoop in and arbitrage your savings; no one will make a takeover play for your savings.

I also talked with numerous financial planners on the sly. None made more than a passing reference to my level of savings and how I might increase it. Again, this is understandable but hardly tolerable: Financial planners don't make any commissions by my saving more money. They make their money when I buy their investment products.

But for young people savings is the key. This may be obvious, but I don't think so. Why do I think savings is the key? Let's look at the ways you can get rich:

1. Hit the lottery.
2. Your grandfather, David Rockefeller, leaves you several zillion dollars.
3. While on vacation in Hawaii, your spouse unburies treasure.
4. Invent Lotus 1-2-3, the Apple Computer, or the VCR.
5. Become the Beatles.
6. You invest your money in wise investments and, over time, it multiplies.

As you can tell, all my ways of getting rich are slightly facetious, save the last. You've got to work at making money. This isn't to say that working at your job will make you rich. You may be comfortable, but not rich. Investing will be your source for riches. If you invest, however, you must invest a significant amount for the return to be meaningful.

More Than Just Pennies

At one time I was involved in the market for low-price, so-called penny, stocks. These stocks, which trade in the Over-the-Counter market, are usually bought for less than one dollar per share. Potential investors would come up to me and say, "I've got a whole stack of pennies—can you do something for me?" This was inevitably followed by a deep "Har-dee-har-har" belly laugh. After the second time I heard this I didn't find it quite as amusing as the tellers always seemed to think I would. But it does highlight a good point.

If you invest 100 pennies and the return on investment is 100 percent, you've earned 100 pennies—one dollar. Big deal. Even if the return on investment was 500 percent, your 100 pennies would only multiply into a megastack of pennies—500 of 'em, $5.00. Again . . . big deal.

But if you had $10,000 to invest, then the 100 percent return would be meaningful—you would now have an additional $10,000. In other words, you've got to have a stack of cash for an investment to be worthwhile.

Furthermore, many investments require hefty commissions, so you need a large investment across which to amortize the sales charge. In the stock market the cheapest commission will cost you around $50. Hence, your investment must exceed $50 by a considerable amount, or else your investment will cost you too much from the beginning. Likewise, in real estate, you generally need at least 15 percent of the purchase price—if not 20 percent—which will amount to at least $10,000.

No Socking In the Mattress

Saving your money is a boring subject. It's not about Broadway shows, it's not about Jaguar XKE's, nor is it about shopping-center limited partnerships with 3-to-1 payouts. To most people, saving means socking away the cash in a 5¼ percent passbook savings account. Nothing could be further from the truth. Saving refers to placing your assets—your money—into some account or investment that promises a return. "Promises" is the operative word here. It doesn't and shouldn't *assure* a return—it need only hold out the promise.

For example, I currently hold much of my liquid assets in a mutual security fund that purchases and holds only tax-free municipal bonds. Interest earned on this account is free from federal taxation. I can write checks against this account, which currently pays an after-tax return of 8 percent. I call this saving and investing.

Savings then represents an allocation of your assets into an investment that promises a return. That's it: a return. Before you can get into any fancy high-horsepowered, high-octane investment vehicles, you've got to have some money to invest. We turn now to finding you that money.

Account Mania

If you're like many people that I spoke with, you have credit cards, cash reserve accounts, savings accounts, expense accounts, and checking accounts. At any one time, though, it's hard to pinpoint exactly how and where you stand. You don't know if you're ahead, behind, upside down, or what. In this chapter we will go through the exercise to determine:

1. Where your money goes,
2. How much money you are currently spending,
3. And how much you're not spending, i.e., saving

Remember, the cornerstone of our plan is to buy a home or to achieve the goal we determined in the last chapter. To do this, you'll undoubtedly need a sizable down payment. We turn now to inflows and outgoes—your income and your expenses. At the end of the month, do you have any left over? My aim is to zero in on those expenses over which you have some control. Begin now.

Monthly Income Report

1. Salary $_____
   - Taxes, Social Security, and Other
     Deductions $_____
2. = Net Take-Home Pay $_____

Monthly Fixed Expenses

Rent or Mortgage Payment (include
maintenance) $_____
Student Loans $_____
Car Payments $_____
Utilities (not including telephone) $_____
Other Loan Payments (not credit cards) $_____
Child-Care Expenses $_____
Health Insurance $_____
Other (describe)* $_____
Other (describe)* $_____
Other (describe)* $_____

3. Total Fixed Expenses $_____
4. Total Take-Home Pay Less Fixed
   Expenses (Item 2 minus item 3) $_____
   What Percent Is This of Your Take-Home
   Pay? (Item 4 divided by item 2) _____%
   What Percent Are Your Fixed Expenses of
   Your Take-Home? (Item 3 divided by item
   4) _____%

* Make sure these so-called "other" are truly expenses over which you have
absolutely no control, that you'd sooner die for before shelving.

We now know how much you could theoretically save. Of course you have to eat and do many of the other little things that make life worth living, such as paying laundry bills. The picture above shows you those expenses over which you have virtually no discretion. Of course, in the longer run, you can change these things—for example, by finding a higher-paying job or getting rid of your car. By and large, you have little choice about whether to pay these bills.

Now we come to your variable expenses. These are a little fuzzier and harder to estimate unless you keep fastidious notes. Estimate these now and fill in the recap sheet that follows:

Monthly Variable Expenses

groceries	$_____
eating out at night	$_____
lunch out	$_____
breakfast out	$_____
transportation	$_____
laundry expense	$_____
going out	$_____
house cleaning	$_____
telephone charges	$_____
health club	$_____
household supplies/maintenance	$_____
periodicals	$_____
education (not student loans)	$_____
hobbies	$_____
other	$_____
other	$_____
other	$_____
Total	$_____

Monthly Picture Recap
(copy from previous)

		Percent of Salary
1. Salary	$_____	100%
— Taxes and Other Deductions	$_____	_____
2. = Net Take-Home Pay	$_____	_____
— Expenses:		
3. Fixed	$_____	$_____
4. Variable	$_____	$_____
5. = Savings/Investment	$_____	$_____

What Percent of Your Take-Home Is Your
Savings? (Item 5 divided by item 2)   _____%

What Percent of Your Total Expenses Are
Your Fixed Expenses? (Item 3 divided by
[item 3 + item 4])   _____%

What Percent of Your Total Expenses Are
Your Variable Expenses? (Item 4 divided by
[item 3 + item 4])   _____%

If you haven't done this before, it's probably an eye-opener. Take your total variable expenses and add another 10 percent. I find that people tend to underestimate their monthly discretionary expenses. The "other" category usually encompasses many things that are left out in the heat of filling out the questionnaire. Take the amount that you have left over for savings and investment and multiply it by 12. Can I look in your savings and investment account(s) and find that much money? If so, congratulations.

If not, the "irregular expense" is probably to blame. You're watching your pennies, and then the big blow—call it Bloomingdale's fall sale, call it the annual vacation to the Continent, call it whatever you like, but there it is—a golden opportunity to spend a big wad of cash. Our planning exercise is specifically aimed at eliminating the "irregular expense."

Let's put some perspective on the numbers you've painstakingly written down. If you have skipped over the blanks, please fill them in now. You can do it. Just estimate the line items that you're not sure of. The idea is to gain a rough understanding of just where your money goes.

How to Get to $1,000 per Month

If you do not save 10 percent of your gross income per month, we've got some work to do. Don't say "I can't save nearly that much money. My expenses are simply too high." Exactly. That's a tautological argument. The reason you don't save enough money *is* precisely because you spend too much. How much is too much? Anything more than 90 percent of your gross monthly income.

To pare down your expenses, you have to understand where your money goes. In the last section we classified your expenses in two general categories: those that are fixed in the short run and those over which you always have complete control.

Those costs over which you have complete control are the easiest to cut back on. "But I can't stop eating, I can't stop buying clothes, I can't stop going to the health club, I can't cut back on long-distance phone calls, I can't, I can't, and I can't." Oh yes, you can. The general intent is to eliminate those expenses that will have a minimal effect on your life-style.

EASY CUTBACK # 1: Pay Off Your Credit Card and Installment Loans

The first way to cut down on your monthly expenses is to pay off your credit cards. Take the money out of your savings and pay off your credit cards. The only excuse for not doing this is that you don't have enough in savings to cover your credit-card expenses.

If this is the case, cut up your credit cards. You're becoming overwhelmed with all this easy credit. As someone who formerly worked for a bank, I know that the banks make a lot of money from credit cards. You are paying anywhere from 12 percent to 18 percent, or more, for the sheer convenience of buying now and paying later. This is the reverse of the financial life horizon: You buy now and pay even more in the future for the arguable privilege of having it now.

If you pay off your credit cards, you'll join a select few, the group of people who have gained control of their finances. The vast majority of credit-card holders in this country pay off only the minimum required each month. Conversely, a tiny minority understand (and act on this understanding) that credit cards make much money for the banks. These people pay off the total outstanding balance.

If you need a credit card for record-keeping in your work or your business, then get a credit card solely for business use and stick to that commitment. There are certain credit cards that are not really credit cards—in fact, they're really charge cards. These require you to pay off your balance in full each month, e.g., American Express and Diner's Club.

There is an explicit financial benefit for paying off your credit cards. If you earn, say, 6 percent on your money market account but have to pay someone else 19 percent to use their money, you're in a losing proposition from the word *go*. The only justification for paying exorbitant credit-card interest charges is that the yield you're earning on your investment dollars is greater than the credit-card interest charges. And that yield you earn should be unfluctuating. After all, the credit-card people will charge you the same annual percentage rate come hell or high water.

The same concept holds true for any other outstanding loans you have for consumer purchases—not investments. Your car, for instance. Do you have enough in savings to pay off your car loan? If you do, you should pay it off. That's if—and only if—the interest rate on the loan is higher than what you're earning in a money market fund (which it most likely is).

The only argument for not paying off a loan holds little water:

the rainy-day justification. Certainly one needs to have some money in savings for a rainy day. How much is enough? Well, it depends on what you see as some potential problems: getting the car fixed, a vacation, your need to maintain a large savings balance. There is little justification for keeping large savings balances when you have almost as large a balance for a loan you've taken out. If you do this, you must understand that you're paying for this luxury. How much are you paying? . . . The difference between the interest payment you're making and receiving.

For example, if you have an outstanding credit-card balance of $1,000 and $1,000 in a 6 percent savings account, you pay $120 per year for this allocation between debt and equity. The credit card charges you 18 percent per year, you're earning 6 percent, thus, the difference is 12 percent per year. Multiply that by $1,000 and $120 is the result (see Cases 1 and 2). Is the luxury of having money in your account worth $120 per year to you?

Paying off credit-card or consumer installment loans provides a psychological benefit as well. Your constant concerns—how am I ever going to pay this off? when is this ever going to be paid off?— are lifted. Your mind can now shift to other matters.

Remember, we're trying to pare down your expenses and every little bit counts, e.g., $120 for the pleasure of not paying an expense today that you'll eventually have to pay for anyway. (And if you can't afford to pay off your credit cards, then rip them up. Get out a scissors and cut them in half. You've gone beyond your means.)

Case 1:

Maintaining Credit-Card and Savings Account Balances

	Invested in Savings Account	Owed to Credit-Card Companies
Balance	$1,000	−$1,000
Interest Rate	6%	18%
Interest Earned (Charged)	$60	−$180

Year-End Position +$60−$180 = −$120

Case 2:

Paying Off Credit-Card Balance

	Invested in Savings Account	Owed to Credit-Card Companies
Begin Balance	$1,000	−$1,000
Pay Off Credit w/Savings	−$1,000	+$1,000
Ending Balance	$ 0	$ 0
Interest Rate	6%	18%
Interest Earned (Charged)	0	0

Summary:

In Case 1 You Pay . . . .   −$120

In Case 2 You Pay $0 . . . . $ 0

Benefit for Paying Off Credit Cards = $120

EASY CUTBACK # 2: Eating Out

Another major step that can be taken immediately is cutting down on your eating-out expenses. It's an insidious drain every time you sidle up to a restaurant and order pasta primavera, mesquite-grilled tuna steaks, or some other trendy new food. Even if you don't eat trendy nouvelle cuisine, burgers and steaks can add up just as quickly.

I don't care where you live, I don't care how cheap the restaurants are, I don't care how many hours you work, and I don't care about your aptitude in the kitchen. Eating out is the young professional's number-one drain. The cost dynamics of eating out are intense and prohibitive. When you worked up your expense sheets in the previous chapter, you came up with an estimate for the total cost of eating out. I bet you underestimated it.

Eating out serves two purposes in our lives: sustenance and social needs. Eating out also provides us with the opportunity to spend three to four times what it would cost to eat at home. And if you go in for nouvelle cuisine, you're looking at six to eight times what it would cost at Chez Your House. And what about American regional? Who would ever have thought they could charge $18 for pot roast?

Correcting this problem requires a little discipline and planning. If you go to the supermarket and spend freely, that's fine. The minute you sit down to a home-cooked meal, almost regardless of what it is, you save money.

Limit the number of times you go out at night each week. It should be at least one less, if not half, as many times as you do currently. If you plan a bit and figure out what you can make at home, you're already ahead of the game. "But I work too many hours, I don't have time for that." Bunk. A key to saving money is cutting corners. And eating at home is the fastest and shortest corner there is.

EASY CUTBACK # 3: Pay Yourself

This, again, is one of those things that seem so obvious it's almost trivial. When you get your paycheck, minutes—no, seconds— after that twice-monthly event, write a check to your saving and investing account. At the end of the month you won't be tempted to spend money previously earmarked for saving. By the way, if you don't have a separate account for saving money as opposed to spending, you should open one up immediately. In the chapter on mutual funds we'll look at some of the various vehicles I suggest for just this purpose.

An even easier way to accomplish this is to have the money removed automatically from your paycheck before you even see it. Many companies have savings plans: Sign up. Or have your bank automatically deduct a specified amount from your account each month. If you bank by computer, set up a recurring payment schedule that automatically deducts 10 percent from your paycheck. If you never see the money, you'll be less likely to spend it. As a direct consequence, you cut back on your spending. Almost all the people I consider successful at saving employ this contrivance that helps them save money. You should do this as well. (If you've signed up for checking overdraft protection from your bank, you must train yourself not to go into a negative position. This overdraft protection can negate the whole purpose of the enforced saving program.)

The Now-It's-Not-So-Easy Cutbacks

We spent the last few pages reviewing ways of cutting your expenses easily. Now let's turn to more engaging methods of cutting back. We'll look at reducing both the fixed and variable expenses.

Among your fixed-expense category we find: (1) your rental or mortgage charges, (2) your utilities, (3) your student loans, (4) your car payments, (5) your child-care expenses, (6) life and medical insurance, and not much else.

1. In the next chapter we delve into your housing/living costs. Accordingly, we'll table that important subject until the next chapter.
2. For your utilities, when you buy appliances, look for energy-efficient ones.
3. If you have outstanding student loans and you chance upon a windfall, don't, under most circumstances, pay it off. You might think that it would be nice to get that out of the way so you wouldn't have to worry about it each month. Clean the slate and all that stuff. Your loan has a low interest rate, probably between

4 and 9 percent. You can most likely find an investment that will pay, with absolute certainty, a rate higher than what you're paying on your student loans. Hence, if you can find an investment that pays more than your loan, you'll be coming out ahead. (This is not abusing the student-loan programs, which were set up to help you finance your education. If you took out the loan and then immediately threw the money into a high-yielding tax-free account, that was abusive. However, if you used the money to finance your education and now you're sticking to the repayment schedule, you need not feel immoral about not paying off the loan faster than you are required to.)

4. Car payments: As you know by now, I'm a strong advocate of not paying interest charges *except* for investment or leveraging purposes. Any time you pay interest charges for consumption purposes, it's money down the drain. Interest charges allow you to fly now and pay later. Why not pay now and fly farther later?

5. Child-care expenses: See if your company will pick up any expenses.

6. Life insurance: If you're single and no one depends on you financially, don't pay a cent for life insurance. Why would you need it if you died? If you have a family, buy only term insurance. Term insurance simply provides you with protection if you die or become incapacitated. There are no savings or investment features with term insurance. At your age, term insurance will be cheap.

Insurance salespeople will try to sell you what is called whole life insurance, and that can go by other names today, e.g., universal life. This insurance provides you with some investment/savings benefits. Without a doubt, you're better off buying investments from those who sell investments and buying insurance from someone who sells insurance.

The Variable Expenses

Your variable expenses are funny sorts of things. At first, they start out as luxuries, and then, almost before you know it, they become necessities. You didn't mind watching *M*A*S*H.* in black and white until you bought a color set, and now you'll never go back. When you lived on the third floor you didn't know you were missing the view, but by the time you could afford the tenth or twentieth floor, you wouldn't consider not having a view.

Once we become comfortable with a luxury, it becomes a necessity. I wrote my first book on a simple electric typewriter. Today I wouldn't even consider writing on a typewriter. Of course my word processor is about ten times more costly than an electric typewriter.

Think back to your list of variable or discretionary spending expenses that we established in this chapter. Which of those expenses did you incur in college? Probably very few of them. And the ones you did have in college didn't come close to scaling the heights that these expenses do today. Do you have someone come in to do the cleaning? . . . You didn't worry about a clean villa in your college days. The health club? Laundry expenses? Jeans don't need dry cleaning. You probably spent less money on groceries. Macaroni and cheese (Kraft Dinner to aficionados) doesn't make as big a dent in the budget as do smoked mozzarella and sun-dried tomatoes.

Today, with that big income of yours, you're spending a lot more on day-to-day living. You're spending more money on things you would never even have considered just a few short years ago. I say "It's time to go back to college" with your spending patterns.

I've repeated the list of variable expenses we developed earlier. This time, though, I've broken it into three columns. The first item is "Total Variable Expense," which you should copy from your calculations on page 67.

A Further Look at Your Variable Expenses

Item	Total	Absolute	Some Discretion
Total Variable Expense (from above)	_____		
groceries	_____	_____	_____
eating out at night	_____	XXXXXX	_____
lunch out	_____	_____	_____
breakfast out	_____	XXXXXX	_____
transportation	_____	_____	_____
laundry expense	_____	_____	_____
going out	_____	XXXXXX	_____
house cleaning	_____	_____	_____
telephone charges	_____	_____	_____
health club	_____	XXXXXX	_____
household supplies/ maintenance	_____	_____	_____
periodicals	_____	XXXXXX	_____
education (not student loans)	_____	_____	_____
hobbies	_____	_____	_____
other _____	_____	_____	_____
other _____	_____	_____	_____
other _____	_____	_____	_____
Total	_____	_____	_____

In this chart I have taken the liberty of deciding that some expenses, despite what you may think, are not necessary. Add up the numbers you have in the "Some Discretion" column. Now we know the amount that could potentially end up in your savings account each month.

How much do you already save each month? Add that to the "Total—Some Discretion" number we've just calculated. This is the potential sum that you would add to your net worth on a monthly basis. However, you save only what you save. You can now see where the fat is, based on the table above. Below are some more ideas about how you can implement a cost-control program.

Bank Charges

I once worked for the largest bank in the country. The managers of this bank, along with those of other profitable banks, aren't stupid. They're in business to make money from their customers. In a perfect world you'd go only to the bank that best served your needs. It would provide you a service. In turn, you would pay the exact amount necessary to satisfy your banking needs.

Well, this isn't a perfect world. The bank you go to is the one that's most convenient, not necessarily the one with the lowest charges. You can lower those charges without much aggravation. By keeping a minimum balance in some account at your bank, you can get your checking charges waved. Let's say you keep, on average, $200 in your checking account. Sure, it fluctuates widely, from the day you get your paycheck to the end of the month, when it drops precipitously close to zero. But, on average, you maintain a $200 balance.

Your bank charges you $5.00 per month for normal account maintenance, the checks you write, and for your withdrawals at the automatic teller machines. Five dollars doesn't seem like much, and you pay it. Over the course of the year, you pay $60 to your bank for their services.

In other words, the bank earns 30 percent on your money:

$$\frac{\$5.00 \times 12 \text{ months}}{\text{Average daily balance}} = \frac{\$60}{\$200} = 30\%$$

The bankers have access to (and use) your funds, and essentially, they charge you 30 percent for the privilege. Even if your average balance is higher, say, $500, you still pay 12 percent for the bank's use of your funds.

Think of it this way: You can earn 12 to 30 percent by simply not paying those charges. That's a great return—one that can be had by a simple action. Call up your bank and find out what you need to do to eliminate those charges. Most require you to keep a minimum balance of anywhere from $1,000 to $2,500 in some account. Or else some simply require that you keep your checking-account balance above a certain level. If it ever dips below that amount—even if only for a second—then you pay the charges. Don't pay those charges.

Some banks offer credit lines that are attached to your checking account. These credit lines, sometimes called overdraft protection, allow your checking-account balance to go negative. In essence, you take out a loan every time you have insufficient funds to cover your checks. These provide a valuable service. On the other hand, they are tempting. "Sure, I can pass this check. Even though I don't have the money right now, my credit line will cover it," you say.

If you deposit money, some banks will use those funds to pay off your credit line and the residual goes into your checking account. Others, though, simply put all the money into your checking account and allow the credit line to keep bumping along. All the while you keep paying interest charges. My dictate with credit cards holds here as well: Pay off that revolving line as soon as you can. There's no need to pay needless charges.

You shouldn't even consider keeping more money in your checking account than is absolutely necessary. If you're clever about managing your cash flow and using your bank's automatic transfer programs, you can actually manage your cash the way big corporations do. I'm not talking about shipping your money back and forth between continents to get the best interest rate possible. It's simpler than that. If you know you have your mortgage or rent payment to make at the first of the month, you can instruct your bank to transfer that amount to your checking account from a money market account or mutual fund the day before. Over a year, it can make a difference.

Banks, of course, also offer credit cards. If you didn't heed my advice about paying off your credit-card outstanding balance, and end up paying interest charges, you should minimize the interest charges you pay. You can do this by calling a few banks to find out the interest rate they charge. Also, determine if you get charged interest from:

1. the day the charge hits your account,
2. the day your statement is mailed to you,
3. the outstanding balance after you have made your monthly payment.

Find out what the bank's annual fees are. These vary widely. Remember, you're not doing them a favor—pay as little as possible.

While we're thinking about credit cards, let's talk about the new prestige cards. Visa has them. MasterCard has them. And the granddaddy of them all, American Express, now has two. The green card, AMEX's first card, was notable because of its selective income requirements. But, when AMEX relaxed its eligibility requirements for the Green Card, the firm began offering the Gold Card. When AMEX decided a more prestigious card was needed, the Platinum Card was born. You may be important enough for a Green, or Gold Card, but do you have what it takes to get a Platinum Card? went the reasoning of the American Express honchos.

I recently received a letter from John C. Sutphen—he's a senior vice-president of American Express. He told me that I *"deserved* to join the select group of individuals who carry the Gold Card." He considers me "select" because the card is not offered to most people. Putting his arm figuratively over my shoulder, he confided to me, "Frankly, that is one of the satisfactions of acquiring the Gold Card. It makes a most eloquent statement when you present it." The final boost to my already-inflated ego came when he said to me, in a hushed tone, that the card "says you are someone special—successful, self-confident, whose style of living requires very special privileges." Yes, the Gold Card would afford me the privilege of carrying around a gold-colored piece of plastic in my wallet and knowing that every Tom, Dick, and Harry wouldn't have the same piece of plastic in their pockets. I turned Mr. Sutphen of AMEX down.

With these prestige cards, who are you trying to impress? The clerk who runs the card through a machine? The waiter who takes the card to the telephone verification machine? These prestige cards are just absurd. Credit-card companies try to differentiate the normal credit-card user from the upscale users. If your company pays for your credit card, then fine. Let your company be unwise shoppers. But since we're aiming to cut down your spending in ways that will have little impact on your life-style, getting rid of the so-called prestige cards and turning them in for "vanilla" charge cards is one simple step.

To be fair, these cards do carry additional benefits. If these are services you specifically desire, then fine. But more than likely it would be cheaper for you to buy these services directly.

Telephone Charges

With deregulation changing the face of the telecommunications industry, it's difficult to detail how you can save money on your telephone expenses. I have found that most people pay exorbitant long-distance charges. There are some simple steps you can take, however, to reduce your overall phone charges.

No, I'm not going to ask you to stop reaching out and touching your loved ones. The easiest way to reduce your charges is to look at your phone bills and figure out where the bulk of your long-distance charges are made. Armed with that information, call up Sprint, MCI, AT & T and any other long-distance carriers in your vicinity. Find out how much they charge for calls to that location after five o'clock. Which one charges the lowest? Go with that one. It'll take all of five minutes to establish an account with that company.

Don't rent your phone from the phone company. If you do rent now, cancel it. Go out and buy your own phone. Every place in town now sells telephones, and the rental or lease charges make absolutely no sense.

Brokerage Fees

Do you trade stocks actively? If so, the only justification for keeping your account at a full-service brokerage house is if you need a broker to make stock suggestions and if you like their research reports. If you make your own investment decisions, then go with a discount broker. That step alone could increase your returns significantly. You could wind up paying only half as much for commissions.

For example, I did a little comparison shopping. You could buy $2,000 worth of stock from Merrill Lynch for a commission charge of $60. You could also buy that same amount from Muriel Siebert & Company—a small New York discount brokerage—for $35. Don't forget, though, that you've got to sell that stock someday. And for that service the brokerage houses kindly take a commission again, $60 vs. $35.

Let's see what that does to your return. The shares, I assume, appreciate 10 percent to $2,200. Your broker works for Merrill Lynch and you pay $120 in commissions. Conversely, if your order taker worked for Siebert & Company, you'd have to pay only $70. Your basis—what the investment cost you—would be either $2,120 or $2,070. You sold at $2,200. You earned either $80 or $130. The rate of return is either 3.8 or 6.3 percent, depending on where you bought and sold the stock (see Chart 12):

CHART 12

Stock Purchase
Discount vs. Full-Service Brokerage

	Full-Service Brokerage	Discount Brokerage
Stock Cost 200 Shares @ $10	−$2,000	−$2,000
Commission to Buy	−$60	−$35
Commission to Sell	−$60	−$35
Basis	−$2,120	−$2,070
Stock Sale 200 Shares @ $11	$2,200	$2,200
Gain	$80	$130
Rate of Return (gain/basis)	3.8%	6.3%

You say you don't buy stocks, you don't care about this. When you save up enough money you will be buying stocks. This may be a part of your savings and investment program. As shown, a simple understanding of the mechanics of stock purchase can do a lot to increase your return. Similarly, this can reduce your risk. Conversely, say your stock headed south—it went down 10 percent to $1,800. Your loss will be magnified by the amount you paid in commissions, −15 percent vs. −13 percent. Also, buy stocks in round lots, that is, in combinations of 100. This will save on your transaction costs as you won't pay odd-lot charges.

Paradigm Shift

We've just gone through some exercises to determine how much you save and how you can improve on that amount. Saving money is an art. It requires thought. It requires diligence. The aim, very simply, is to increase the amount and the percentage of your total take-home pay that is saved and invested. I hope to make you think about saving and investing in a different way than you probably do. Call it brainwashing, call it logic. I call it a paradigm shift.

A paradigm is a world view. It's the way we think things are and the way things should be. It's a mind-set. For example, the theory of evolution is a paradigm. It's a pair of lenses through which we view and explain the world. While evolution is still mildly controversial, 125 years ago it was an extremely radical concept. It upset the accepted notion that God had created a natural order, "a hierarchy of obligations and mutual dependencies throughout nature."* This overriding paradigm can be used to explain why society acts as it does. Many actions we take are predicated on and justified by natural selection: We claw our way to the top because only the strongest survive.

The recent innovation of silicon circuits has also caused a paradigm shift. Mechanical moving parts and transistors are no longer necessary to process information. Silicon circuits have opened whole new vistas for electrical engineers to solve problems. For example, to write these words twenty years ago, I would have sat down with a mechanical typewriter and pounded away at the keys to produce a written word. Today my written words are mere electrons, pushed, collected, and saved electronically. In the modern world we cannot go a whole day without using a silicon circuit. This, too, represents a paradigm shift, a whole other way of collecting information about the world and making it understandable.

The paradigm shift I require you to undergo has to do with saving money. You must change your thought patterns from that of spender to saver.

In my discussions with people about their spending and saving habits, I initially went into the interviews with the understanding that what people saved today they could spend tomorrow. Saving today represented an opportunity to spend tomorrow. Something new began to emerge. Those people who saved enjoyed saving. Saving was just as much a source of gratification as was, say,

---

* Jeremy Rifkin, *Algeny* (New York: Viking Press, 1983), p. 37.

buying a new VCR. How can that be? How do you get enjoyment and pleasure from not doing something?

But these people *are* doing something. They're saving money. For this select group of people who *do* enjoy saving, saving is an end unto itself. If you're not in the group who can save at least 10 percent of your gross pay, or if you can't save a dime, you've got your work cut out for you. Over the last few pages I've described some simple tricks to save money. Understand that you have to want to save money—that's the bottom line. You gain enjoyment by saving money. You don't have to become a skinflint or a money grubber. Nor, in fact, does it mean you have to become less generous. All it means is that saving money will become part of your financial life-style. An overriding benefit is that as your savings grow, you'll feel less and less constrained by money.

I'm trying to instill two things: (1) that saving and investing don't have to be a matter of hardship and (2) that you need to recondition your mind to make saving and investing your money your primary financial concern. Any time you consider saving and investing a hardship, you're turning yourself into a martyr.

Part of the deal that I made to you at the outset was that my plan wasn't arduous, that it didn't require nerves of steel. And I'm holding to that. Save $50 a month. Save $100 a month. Save something. Once you've begun to change your mind-set, to shift your paradigm, you can begin establishing larger and larger amounts. But until you make that first step, you'll never get anywhere. Remember, the first step is to change the way you think about saving money, not to establish a nest egg of fabulous proportions today. Start with a small amount of money. But save something.

The rest of this book is devoted to determining what you should do with the money that you've saved. We'll look at real estate, the stock and bond markets, and mutual funds. We'll spend a few pages considering taxes. Then it's on to buying your first home.

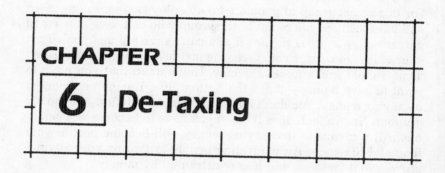

CHAPTER 6 De-Taxing

As you make more and more money, the hope and aim of this book, you'll pay more and more in taxes. In the topsy-turvy world of taxes, where gains are losses and losses are gains, you'll now face the ironically enviable problem of minimizing them. Alas, just like death, there's no such thing as avoiding taxes. But you can postpone them.

The wealthier you become, the more you'll be able to pay for the services of tax experts. Since you're not at that stage yet, you should have a general understanding of tax concepts. Before plunging into the depths of financial planning, we need to clear up several common misperceptions about taxation.

Every financial move you make has tax implications. As financial planner Stanley Cohen writes, "Being tax smart is at the heart of all my planning. Whenever I recommend a move to [my clients], I must always consider the tax consequences first. . . . What is the tax effect going to be?"* There are ways to arrest the growth in your tax payments so that they don't exceed the growth

* Stanley J. Cohen and Robert Wool, *How to Survive on $50,000 to $150,000 a Year* (New York: Penguin Books, 1984), p. 7.

in your income. Your home will be your chief tax dodge, and we'll get to that in the next chapter.

In this short chapter I only want to provide an understanding of some rudimentary concepts behind taxation. Grasping the theory behind taxes is fundamental to personal finance. For instance, even though the top tax rate is 28 percent, someone earning $50,000 will pay only 23 percent in taxes. At the end of this chapter you'll understand how this could be.

The Short and Long of It

To solidify the vocabulary, let's turn to the hypothetical example of Joe College's tax situation before getting into the real world. Joe made $10,000 through part-time jobs. He takes one exemption for himself, which reduces his gross income by $1,900, and he takes the standard deduction, which reduces his gross income by an additional $2,480. That leaves him with his net taxable income. He pays tax on his taxable income. To determine his tax, Joe looks up the tax on his net taxable income in the tax table and fills in the amount. In 1988 Joe pays $495 in federal taxes (see Chart 13).

CHART 13

Gross Income	$10,000
Less Standard Deduction	− $2,480
Less $1,080 for Each Exemption	− $1,080
= Net Taxable Income	$6,440
Tax on $6,440	$495

Out of every taxable dollar he earned, 7.7 cents was paid to the federal government. This means his average tax rate is 7.7 percent. It doesn't mean that Joe's in a 7.7 percent bracket. We'll get to that shortly. Note that I use the term *taxable* dollar. Specifically, this is any income against which the tax tables are applied.

You want to maximize your gross income—that which is not

directly subject to taxation—and to minimize the net income—that which is directly subject to taxation. The government has a select list of items that you can use to reduce your gross income. These items are the deductions that you *itemize* on your tax returns.

The adjustments to income and items that you can deduct include employee business expenses, medical expenses, state and local income taxes, mortgage interest, and casualty and theft losses.

If you have any of these expenses, you can reduce your net taxable income by that amount. To make it worth your while to itemize, you must have at least the amount of the standard deduction in itemizable expenses. Joe College would need at least $2,480 of these expenses to make it worth his while to itemize.

A common misconception is that by reducing your taxes, you'll end up with the money in your pocket. Ninety-nine percent of the time, this is wrong. Instead of paying the money to the IRS, you end up paying the money to someone else, like a bank. (There's an exception to this rule, which I'll discuss in the real estate chapter.)

For example, you can deduct your mortgage interest payments. The more money you spend on mortgage interest, the less your taxable income will be. "Bingo," you say, until you realize that instead of paying the money to the government, you are paying it to the mortgage banker.

The situation is similar when you run up a big medical bill. You say, "Well at least I get to deduct those expenses." That's true, but now instead of paying the money to the government, you've paid that money to a hospital or a doctor. I've often been asked how to beat taxes. You can beat taxes, but you won't have the money in your pocket. Instead, you pay the money to someone else. Your hope is that someday you'll get that money back, i.e., when you make investments.

You can calculate the value of a deduction. It's simply the reduction in your tax burden. The value of the tax deduction to you, though, is not the cost of the item. For instance, your mortgage payment is tax deductible. That almost sounds as if you'll reduce the size of your tax burden, dollar for dollar, by the amount of your mortgage payment. That's not it. To calculate its true dollar worth to you, you need to know your tax bracket.

Tax Clamps

I always thought that the tax people came up with such colorful language. The words *tax burden* conjure up images of donkeys, asses, and some poor Sisyphus, condemned to an eternity of filling out 1040s. The words *tax brackets* suggest the pincerlike hands on some overzealous, red-faced, lobster-shelled IRS tax accountant. The concept of tax brackets, while frequently bantered around, is widely misunderstood.

The amount you pay in taxes divided by your total income is your average tax rate. The additional tax you pay on an additional dollar of income is determined by your tax bracket. An analogy will make this clearer.

Think of it this way. At 6:00 this morning you walked out of your house. You got into your car. You set your odometer to 000,000. By 6:05 you had warmed up the car, opened the garage, backed out of your driveway, and just entered the street. You drove cautiously, fifteen to twenty miles per hour, through the predawn haze. At 6:15 you got on the expressway. You cruised along at sixty-five miles per hour. After fifteen minutes you looked down at your odometer. You'd traveled twenty miles.

You'd traveled twenty miles in the half hour since you walked out your door. Thus, your average speed was forty miles per hour. At the beginning of your daily trip, you were walking, then you were speeding along at twenty mph. Finally, you were traveling at a rate of sixty-five miles per hour.

And so it is with tax brackets. In 1988 the first $17,850 you earn will be taxed at the rate of 15 percent. When you start earning more than that amount you'll be charged at the rate of 28 percent. Your "rate" of taxation will have increased from 15 percent to 28 percent, just as your rate of speed increased from twenty to sixty-five miles per hour.

Let's say you earn $17,850 in 1988. This means you will pay 15 percent of this amount, or $2,678, in federal taxes. If you earn twice as much, $35,700, you will pay 15 percent on the first $17,850, or $2,678, and 28 percent on the second $17,850, or $4,998. Your total tax bill would be $7,676.

Of every dollar you earn past $17,850, you'll pay 28 cents of it to the government. The following chart should simplify this (see Chart 14):

CHART 14

Income +	Additional Income	= Total Income	Tax +	Additional Tax	= Total Tax
		15% Bracket			
$17,650 +	0	= $17,650	$2,647 +	0	= $2,647
$17,650 +	$100	= $17,750	$2,647 +	$15	= $2,663
$17,650 +	$200	= $17,850	$2,647 +	$30	= $2,678
		28% Bracket			
$17,850 +	$100	= $17,950	$2,678 +	$28	= $2,706
$17,850 +	$200	= $18,050	$2,678 +	$56	= $2,734

This is based on the brackets as envisioned for 1988 as I write this. The leaders of the country may decide to change the brackets by the time you read this. However, the concept that a higher rate is applied after a certain income point will remain. To determine your personal tax burden, simply use one of the formulas below (see Chart 15):

There's more to it than this, however. You must add in the calculation for your state and local taxes as well. Just like the federal tax system, most states have a graduated system as well. For this reason, in determining your actual tax bracket, you must include your state and local bracket as well. For example, residents of New York City can end up paying an additional 18 percent of their income to the state and city governments. Some states and cities don't have an income tax. In determining your tax bracket, you obviously must include the state and local effect as well.

CHART 15

Single Individuals
15% × $17,850 + 28% × (Your Income − $17,850) = Your Tax

Married Individuals Filing Joint Returns
15% × $29,750 + 28% × (Your Income − $29,750) = Your Tax

Heads of Households
15% × $23,900 + 28% × (Your Income − $23,900) = Your Tax

Married Individuals Filing Separately
15% × $14,875 + 28% × (Your Income − $14,875) = Your Tax

Why Brackets Matter

Taxes and brackets should be considered before you make any investment decision. In 1988, more than likely, you'll be in at least a 28 percent tax bracket. If you invest in a savings and investment account paying 6 percent, you should understand that because of taxes you're not really earning 6 percent.

Let's say you invest $1,000 in this account. After a year's time of compounding interest, the account will earn $62. When you fill out your tax form, in the interest-earned section you enter $62 (see Chart 16). This will be *added* to your salary to determine your net taxable income. The additional increase in interest earnings of $62 causes your taxes to increase by $17 (28 percent of $62). Conversely, you get to keep $45. Your after-tax return then is:

$$\frac{\$45}{\$1,000} = 4.5\%$$

CHART 16

	Without Interest Earnings	With Interest Earnings	Difference
Salary Income	$27,560	$27,560	——
+ Interest Income	–0–	$62	$62
– Deductions	–$3,560	–$3,560	–0–
= Net Taxable Income	$24,000	$24,062	$62
– Tax Owed	–$4,400	–$4,417	–$17
= After-Tax Income	$19,601	$19,645	$45

The same concept holds true in determining the value of a tax deduction. Say you incur $100 in deductible medical expenses. Your $100 medical expense reduces your net taxable income by the same amount, $100. That means you'll reduce your taxes by $100 times your tax bracket, or 28 percent, or $28. Here's how it works (see Chart 17):

CHART 17

	Without Medical Deduction	With Medical Deduction	Difference
Salary Income	$27,560	$27,560	–0–
– Medical Expenses	–0–	–$100	–$100
– Deductions	–$3,560	–$3,560	–0–
= Net Taxable Income	$24,000	$23,900	–$100
– Tax Owed	–$4,400	–$4,372	$28
= After-Tax Income	$19,601	$19,529	–$72

As you can see, by paying out $100 in medical expenses, you save $28 in taxes. However, comparing your net income with and without the medical deduction, you're still $72 worse off by paying the medical bill.

And that's the thing about deductions: Even though deductions reduce your tax bill, at some time you still have to shell out the money. In this instance you paid $100 to your doctor. This reduced your tax bill by $28. You were out $72. Conversely, if you hadn't had the medical bill, your taxes would have been $28 higher but you'd have $72 more in your pocket.

Mush!

From this chapter the two points to be recognized are that (1) you're in a tax bracket that's probably higher than you think and (2) you cannot avoid paying taxes. You can reduce your tax bill, but then, as pointed out, you end up paying the money to someone else.

SECTION

C HOME PURCHASE

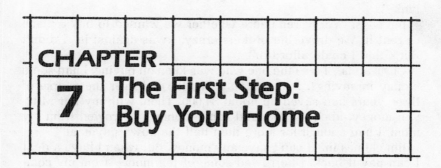

CHAPTER

7 The First Step: Buy Your Home

Two twenty-five-year-old guys, Chris Remington and Jim Dorian, explained their financial prowess to me in the apartment they own in Park Slope, Brooklyn, while we quaffed some brews. You'll remember from earlier in the book that Chris and Jim had turned an $11,000 down payment into a potential gain of $20,000 in the space of a year. Their apartment is in what we might call a "changing neighborhood." The apartment building right next to theirs has bricked-up windows. On the corner is the skeleton of a building that looks like it might have been imported from Beirut. Despite this, right across the street from the "Hotel Beirut" is an old factory building that has been recently gutted and restored as a luxury condo. In it one-bedroom apartments sell for $185,000.

Their two-bedroom apartment had been purchased a year ago for $110,000. They put 10 percent, or $11,000, down. When I spoke with them they told me that the apartment next door, a mirror image of theirs, had recently sold for $130,000. In other words, they, too, stood to gain $20,000 on an $11,000 investment. Ah, the magic of leverage.

Chris says, "We had each been paying $250 per month to rent up in the Bronx, and we wanted to move down to Manhattan. But we looked around at some of the prices and at the small spaces we'd have had to live in and had second thoughts. Then some broker said, 'Why don't you buy a place, over yonder in Brooklyn?' "

Jim says, "We weren't sure whether we wanted to buy a place or rent it. We drove the brokers crazy. I was against it—I didn't think that I could afford it."

Chris adds, "I was the one who was keen on buying. I had some money in savings. I save $100 a month, and over the course of three years had saved up about $4,000. Then, with my Bar Mitzvah money, about $3,000, and some money I borrowed from my mom, I had enough for more than half the down payment."

Jim chimes in, "I can't save any money. But when I have a debt I can pay it back. I borrowed some of the money from my company, some of the money from a bank, and came up with $4,000." (Typically, though, mortgage lenders will not allow any or all of the down payment to come from borrowed funds.)

"It sounds like Chris had too much," I said, calculating, "and Jim didn't have enough to split it straight down the middle?"

"Exactly," Chris says. "Because of that, we originally split it 65/35. An accountant worked up the numbers for us. I paid for 65 percent of the equity and the tax-deductible expenses. For the non-tax-deductible expenses, we split it 50/50. Our view was that for the non-tax-deductible expenses, we should split it down the middle." (Very shortly we'll discuss what home-purchase expenses are deductible from your taxes.)

Jim explains, "I knew I couldn't afford the whole 50 percent. But Chris and I have been friends for a long time. If there's anybody I would trust with an investment, it is Chris. We decided to arrange it this way. After a few months, though, I decided it would be better to share it 50/50. I figured out the expenses he had incurred up to that point and started paying Chris that amount for the additional increment. I've been paying him on an accelerated schedule to earn my 50 percent share. Starting next month, I'll own 50 percent of it."

Chris and Jim are gregarious, enthusiastic fellows. Chris sells business forms and Jim is a research analyst. Chris's resume states that he was the top seller of business forms in his region and, among other things, he was the mascot for the basketball team at UCLA. In the few short years since the two have graduated from college, they have been able to parlay their meager savings into a sizable investment, which has already grown substantially in value. Jim says, "Our goal is to make one investment in real estate each year."

Smart People Buy Their Own Homes

In these chapters we turn to real estate: researching it, exploring it, investing in it, and buying it. From our perspective, there are two kinds of real estate: the kind you buy to live in and the kind you buy to invest in. This isn't to say, though, that the place you live in shouldn't be considered an investment.

My aim in this chapter is simple: to instruct you in the mechanics of finding, buying, and financing real estate. The first step is to know in your soul that it can be done. We'll look at why you think you can't possibly buy a home or condominium. We'll knock down those arguments one-two-three. We'll look at the reasons you can buy a place. Then we'll turn to the nuts and bolts: choosing the right kind of place, finding a mortgage banker, and structuring the financing package for your house.

In conducting my field research for this book I observed that all the people who were on their way to building a substantial nest egg also happened to own the place they lived in. These people knew that buying a home or condominium was, and continues to be, the right thing to do. It pulls you out of the black hole of rent.

Getting Out of the Black Hole

"From colonial times, Americans [have] preferred their own backyards to more public places. Ever since, owning a home has been a reward for thrift and industry and a cornerstone of American life,"* says the almanac of moving up, *Money* magazine. Today a home is increasingly seen as an investment, a springboard

---

* "Your Home," *Money Guide: Your Home* (New York: Time Inc., 1985), p. 9.

from which larger investments can be made. Continuing to rent your home simply delays the inevitable and is a costly mistake.

Rent is one item in your expense budget that is at the same time both necessary and discretionary. You have to pay for the place you live in. You face a choice: Buy a place and invest in it through your mortgage payments or rent a place and never see that money again. By continuing to rent, you're throwing good dollars away down the black hole of rent.

It's difficult to find a financial argument that points to renting over buying. *The New York Times* tried a few years ago. One young couple, the paper noted, bought their house after renting it for three years. The couple, Dane and Elese Wright, who lived in Hartford, Connecticut, "made the commitment cautiously."

"We lived in apartments for a long time and were afraid to take the risks involved in buying a house," Dane said. He added, "It's a very intimidating experience. Besides, we weren't sure we were going to stay here, and, if we did, the neighborhood was in transition, and we wanted to see which way it eventually went." The implication was that the Wrights, by procrastinating, somehow had made a wise decision.

The New York Times said that "while tax accountants and financial planners concur that, in general, home ownership remains one of the best investments a consumer can make, they also agree that, in some cases, renting may be the better choice."

Hardly! According to the *Times,* renting was preferred over buying by those people who were:

1. going to die,
2. going to move,
3. not in need of much space.

The article claimed that if rents were cheap enough, it made more sense to rent than to buy. For this to be a financially solvent argument, your after-tax interest payments have to be more than your rental payments. Furthermore, when you sell your home, more than likely you will enjoy a gain that you would not earn if you continued to rent. The Wrights were simply nervous about making the decision.* Let's look at someone who knew right from the start that renting was the wrong decision.

Maureen Bruce, who just turned thirty, works in the commercial real estate business in Dallas. Maureen graduated from the University of Denver with a B.S. in Management in 1979. She moved to Dallas and found work at a real estate consulting firm.

Me: What kind of work were you doing?
Maureen: I did market research. I was doing the research on commercial real estate deals. I wasn't intimidated by the work. I was fascinated by the subject. I learned about real estate. By the time my work was completed, I usually knew more about the particular deal and the economics of the situation than anyone in the firm.
Me: How much were you making?
Maureen: I started at $10,000 per year.
Me: How much did you have in the bank when you got out of school?
Maureen: About $5,000.
Me: Tell me about your first investment.
Maureen: I bought my first condo in 1982 for $79,000. It was a two-bedroom place, 950 square feet. By that time my firm had increased my salary to $25,000.
Me: How long did it take you to find the place?
Maureen: Essentially, it took me several years. Right around the time I moved to Dallas, interest rates went through the roof. While I had enough for a down payment, I couldn't qualify for a loan. I looked for two years to find this place. Finally, I found a bank that would sell a mortgage to me. I took out a gradually escalating, nonqualifying assumable loan. ["Gradually escalating" means that the interest rate charged on the loan moves up at prespecified intervals until it settles at some determined rate. "Nonqualifying" means that the person who takes over the loan doesn't have to receive approval from the bank.] My gradually

---

* "Renting Is Right for Some," by Barbara Aarsteinsen, *The New York Times, Personal Finance,* section 12, September 29, 1985, p. 35.

escalating loan started out at 11 percent, moved to 12 percent, and 13 percent, and finally settled at 14 percent for the term of the loan. This is not the traditional adjustable-rate loan, which fluctuates with moves in market interest rates. This was more like a fixed-rate loan, which is fixed for the duration of the loan according to a prespecified contractual agreement. This way I knew how much money I needed to earn as it increased.

Me: Were you able to afford it?

Maureen: The mortgage payments, condo fees, and insurance ran $1,000 per month. But I took in a roommate, who paid $300 a month in rent. My after-tax cost for the place was $300 per month.

The import of Maureen's story is that she said she was going to do it—and she went out and did it. Admittedly, it took her several years. She wasn't able to say "I want to buy a place" and then go out the door and sign on the dotted line. She had to plan, scrimp, and save. It took her two years. But she was committed to buying a residence. She took on a roommate, she shopped around for a mortgage, and she did it. And you can, too, though you might fabricate 1,001 reasons why you can't.

Reasons You Can't Buy Your Home

Let's examine some of the reasons you haven't bought a house, condo, or co-op yet:

1. You don't have the money for a down payment.
2. You can't afford the mortgage payments.
3. Your life is changing and you don't want to be tied down to one place.
4. You can't see yourself living in the places you can afford.
5. You don't know what to do.

I would argue that in the long run number 5 is the only valid reason: You don't know how to go about finding a place to buy that you can live in. We'll remedy that problem in this chapter.

Reasons You Can!

Let's look at the reasons you can and should buy your own home or condominium:

1. It's your own.
2. You've saved up some money and you can tap other sources to borrow the rest (e.g., your parents, a bank unsecured credit line).
3. The housing market is soft, and prices aren't increasing nearly as fast as they were in the late 1970s.
4. You need tax deductions.
5. It is by far cheaper to own than to rent.
6. You can always sell the place. You're not landlocked.

The actual decision to do it is clearly the toughest part about buying a house. Once you figure out what you want to do, you'll go ahead and figure out a way to do it. In college did you ever think you just couldn't go in for the test? You crammed all night, passed the test, and eventually got out of college. It's the same with buying a house, you just need to trudge your way through. You'll make mistakes; you'll think that you can't afford it; you'll look at places you think you wouldn't be caught dead in. You'll come up with countless reasons that you can't possibly buy or find a house.

Buying a house doesn't mean the end of the world. It doesn't mean that once and forever you'll be in that place. It doesn't mean you can't ever take a vacation again. It doesn't mean you can't trade up to a nicer house in a nicer neighborhood. It doesn't mean you're giving up any freedom.

What it does mean is simple. You have made a wise decision, one that is not irrevocable. It just takes legwork, and it can be frustrating. Many times you'll just want to throw your hands up in despair. Nevertheless, here's What You Do:

The Steps

1. Open the paper to the real estate section of the classified ads.
2. Determine the minimum number of bedrooms that you'll need.
3. Find some neighborhoods you would consider.
4. Don't worry about the price at first.
5. Call up the broker. Say you want to have a look at the place. Initially, skirt the money issue. Be vague in responding to the broker's questions concerning how much you make, how much you're willing to pay, and how much you'll put down.
6. Go look at the place. Don't show much interest. (You may not have any interest.) The point is to get out and start looking at places. Look at many. This is the largest single investment you'll probably ever make. Spend some time just looking.
7. Find a place you can afford. We'll look at what you can afford shortly.
8. Agree to buy the place, settle on a price, and go to contract.
9. Find a bank where the terms (interest rates and fees) are competitive compared with those at other local banks.
10. Submit a mortgage application.
11. Wait interminably for the application to be approved.
12. Get approval and set a closing date. (A closing is when you, the seller, and all the lawyers and bankers get together to pass the title. The title is the legal document that shows ownership.)
13. Close.
14. Move in. You're done.

That's all there is to it. Getting started is the toughest part. Just remember that all homeowners had to do it for the first time once. And there is a large community of people who are interested in having you buy a home: the real estate brokers, the banks, the sellers of houses, the attorneys. Of course these people all have a self-interest in getting you to buy a house. It is their job to help you understand the process.

Buying the Right One

"How much house can I afford?" is probably the single most pressing concern of future homeowners, but before considering how much you can afford, you need to answer several questions pertaining to your future domicile:

What kind of neighborhood do you want to live in (inner city, suburb, or exurb)?

What kind of dwelling do you prefer (single-family or apartment)?

What age dwelling is more desirable to you (prewar or modern)?

The neighborhood question depends on your own propensities. Would you prefer to live in an up-and-coming neighborhood, one that already up and went, or one that's already on top? How you answer these questions has a dramatic influence on the price you'll pay. For example, it is estimated that a three-bedroom Victorian house would cost around $120,000 in the Boston working-class community of Somerville. In nearby upper-middle-class Belmont, that same bundle of house would cost around $220,000. Location matters.*

Despite the sentiment of this book, your own house is more than an investment—it's a place to live in. You have to be happy with the neighborhood, the surroundings, the structure itself. This is not to say that the investment aspects of a particular home should be overlooked, just be careful that you want to live there.

Basically, there are two choices when it comes to kinds of dwellings: detached single-family dwellings versus multifamily dwellings. In the multifamily category, you'll find duplexes,

* Robert Runde, "The First Step: Picking the Right Location," *Money Guide: Your Home* (New York: Time Inc., 1985), p. 19.

triplexes, quadruplexes, town houses, small and large apartment buildings. Most likely you'd prefer a single-family site. However, you may not be able to afford one in the neighborhood you're looking at. You may have to settle for one of the variants mentioned above.

You also have the choice of a brand-new or existing building. In the condominium market, by and large, you won't be able to find those that have existed for a hundred years and have age-old charm. Condominiums are a relatively new development on the housing scene, although some condominium conversions from older apartments may be available. Condominiums, however, are considerably more affordable.

Single-family homes tend to appreciate in value at a greater rate than condominiums, at least they have in the past. And single-family homes should continue to appreciate faster because there is a glut of condos on the national market relative to single-family houses. Local conditions may dictate otherwise, however, so it is important for you to do your research in all locations where you're considering purchasing a home.

The size of your bankroll will be a major factor in deciding the house or condo you buy. Determine which neighborhoods you can afford and might want to live in. Next, get out the newspaper's classified ad section. Peruse the ads for listings in that neighborhood. Usually the newspaper will divide the ads by sections of town. Sunday is an especially good day for hunting. In addition, some papers designate another day, typically Wednesday, for running exhaustive listings.

In the neighborhood of your choice, hunt through the section and find the prices for houses and condos with the number of bedrooms you've decided upon. Don't let the prices scare you. Asking prices will usually come down 10 percent. Find places that seem within your financial ballpark. (We'll discuss that ballpark shortly.)

More than likely the phone numbers for the places you are interested in will be that of real estate brokers. Call them up and arrange to look at a place. You probably won't buy the first place you look at. What you will do, however, is begin to establish a relationship with a real estate agent. Once this happens the agent will arrange for you to look at other locations.

All agents aren't the same, however. Some have spent their careers in the business, while others have just become agents recently in the hope of picking up a few extra bucks. Your agent will show you as many places as you have time or patience for. Just remember, the only way they make money from you is if they learn what you're looking for and show you the right houses in the right price range. Only then will you buy the house that they show you. You don't have to jump to make a decision. Take your time. Work with several agents.

In fact, you should see a dozen places—if not twenty. The more properties you look at, the more knowledgeable you'll be about the local real estate market. It doesn't take long to learn about prices and value.

William Nickerson, the real estate wizard who turned $1,000 into $5 million (and wrote a book detailing his experiences)—in his spare time—relates this story of his congregation's search for a house for his minister:

"We were charged with finding a home for our minister in the general neighborhood of the church. We could have spent many fruitless meetings discussing price ranges and could have drawn no valid conclusions. We let our wants be known to various realtors. The minister's wife selected seven suitable homes from their listings, enough to take up a full Saturday of shopping. Before we started, none of us had any conception of price levels for the type of home wanted. By the end of this one day's shopping, every member of our committee of five had formulated a solid idea of market prices and values for the quality of home sought."*

Your aim is to become an expert in the marketplace of your choice. The average home buyer today looks at a dozen potential sites. It will become discouraging after you've visited the first few. All the places will begin to meld together, to become a blur. Keep a log that contains the price, the square footage, the loca-

* William Nickerson, *How I Turned $1,000 into Five Million in Real Estate* (New York: Simon and Schuster, 1980), p. 50.

tion, the taxes, the utilities, and what you did and didn't like about the place. The smarter you are about the marketplace— about what price constitutes a value in the type of housing you're looking for—the better buy you'll get and the happier you'll be in the long run.

Of course buying a place in need of a little fixing up is usually cheaper than getting an already-fixed-up one. Early one Sunday morning I flipped on the TV to a non-network channel. A fellow on television described how he had made $35,000 just last week in real estate. His secret? Ah, for that you'd need $19.95 and a Visa or MasterCard. I listened to him for several minutes and learned his secret. He buys run-down property, slaps a few coats of paint on the building, shores up the foundation, and then, apparently, is able to sell the building for several tens of thousand dollars more than he bought it for.

I always, as a general rule, tend to doubt people who sell fantastic rewards over early-Sunday-morning television. Ask Mr. Ponzi. However, there was a valuable point to be gathered from the early-morning broadcast—and you don't need to spend $19.95 on it. The poorer the appearance, the less you'll probably have to pay to buy it. However, you want to avoid buying a building from someone who spent the $19.95 and applied a coat of paint to ready the building for sale. I strongly advise that you hire your own appraiser to evaluate the building to determine whether there are problems that are not immediately apparent to a nonprofessional.

In addition to the general appearance and condition of the home you select, several other factors go into determining its investment value.

1. Location: Move to the best neighborhood you can afford. A cheap place in a desirable neighborhood is a better investment than an expensive place in a run-down neighborhood. If the neighborhood is turning around, you don't want to have to wait too long for the full turnaround to take place. You might enjoy faster-than-average appreciation if you move to a revitalized neighborhood, but there's always the risk that what you "thought was an up-and-coming neighborhood is actually down-and-out."*

2. Schools: Even if you don't have children now, a location with good neighborhood schools is a better value than one that doesn't have comparable schools. To evaluate schools, look at what percentage of graduates go to college and compare local SAT results with national averages. This is an easy, nonsubjective method to determine the quality of schools without having to take the word of the real estate agent.

3. Municipal services: Is the community well kept up? Does it have a history of fair or exorbitant tax increases? Needless to say, you want to stay away from the latter.

4. Crime: Is there too much? Talk to the local police precinct. See if there's a neighborhood crime-watch group. Talk to neighbors.

5. Transportation: Is the site near mass transit, if that is a common mode of transportation in the area? Is it close to major arteries and hubs?

6. Amenities: Is there a full complement of stores in the vicinity?

Although I opted to discuss the factors that go into deciding which house you want before talking about *financing* your home, you really should attack the home purchase on several fronts simultaneously. While searching for a house you should begin to explore financing options. Similarly, you should look for a lawyer.

Going to Contract

Going to contract refers to the signing of a document by seller and buyer that suggests that you, the buyer, will eventually purchase the place and move in. You haven't really bought the place until you go to the meeting where the title passes hands and money is exchanged.

The seller will ask you to put up a percentage of the total price to show your earnestness in buying the place. He may ask you to

* Robert Runde, "The First Step: Picking the Right Location," *The Money Guide: Your Home*, p. 20.

sign a contract. It's only final when you close and money is exchanged. After that point, it's too late.

You should ask a lawyer to review the papers. A lawyer can bargain to change the terms of the contract for you if you question some of the stipulations the seller requests.

The contract specifies the terms of the sale: the down payment you'll make and the price you'll pay. All the terms of the sale should be spelled out in the contract—what the condition of the house will be when you take it over, what will be fixed or left as is, what appliances will be left in the house, and so on.

Obviously, you should make sure all the terms of the contract that can be inspected *are* inspected before the closing. Once the house is sold and you take title, you'll have a hard time convincing the seller to continue making refurbishments. After having gone to contract—you have contractually agreed to buy the residence from the seller—you submit an application to a bank for a mortgage. Now we turn to the critical issue: getting money.

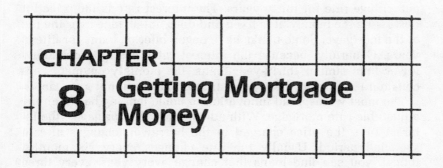

CHAPTER

8 Getting Mortgage Money

To buy a house you'll need to come up with large amounts of capital. More than likely, you'll take out a mortgage—which comes from the French for "dead pledge." You'll pay a certain amount of your own money as the down payment, and you borrow the rest. The only party that cares about how much you put down versus how much is financed is the bank or mortgage lender. Typically, the seller gets all cash for the sale—from both your down payment and the bank's loan.

In this chapter we'll explore the sole issue of paying for your new house. We'll look at mortgages. We'll look at arranging deals. And we'll look at banks. We'll touch briefly on real estate investments at the end. At the conclusion of this chapter you should be a pro at deciphering competitive mortgage information.

The down payment is seen as your commitment to the property you are purchasing. If you didn't put down any of your own money and the bank lent you the entire sum, you could conceivably walk away from the property if you found later that you couldn't afford the payment. The bank does not want to own your property, it just wants to be repaid. Hence, a down payment is seen as your dedication to making the payments and keeping the property in good shape. The more money you offer as a down payment, the smaller your monthly loan payment will be.

In the typical arrangement you borrow the money at a fixed percentage rate for thirty years. The interest rate is the price for borrowing the money. It is fixed and does not change over the life of the mortgage. Some banks have begun offering loans for fifteen years. Generally, because the interest rates are not sufficiently lower than similar thirty-year loans, the monthly payments are considerably higher. As a general rule, these are not good deals.

The most widespread innovation to home lending has been the adjustable-rate mortgage. With adjustable-rate mortgages, the interest rate, the price charged to the borrower, changes after a specified period. Usually the rate changes every six months, though you can find loans that change every year, every three years, or every five years. Typically, the interest rate is calculated by taking a common index of interest rates (six-month Treasury bills are commonly used for this purpose) and adding to that additional percentage points (called the "spread") for the bank's profits and costs. For example, if six-month T-bill rates are 6 percent and the bank spread is 2.5 percent, your mortgage rate would be 8.5 percent. If the T-bill rates dropped to 5 percent, the interest rate you'd be charged is 7.5 percent since the spread is unvarying (see Chart 18):

CHART 18

	Original Loan Date	Six Months Later
6-mo. T-bill	6.0%	5.0%
Spread	2.5%	2.5%
Adjustable Mortgage Rate	8.5%	7.5%

In short, the payment on your mortgage loan may or may not change. If you buy a fixed mortgage, the payment is fixed for the life of the mortgage. For most adjustable-rate mortgages, the payments change every six months or every year.

During the duration of your loan you pay back the money you

borrowed—the principal—and you pay the bank interest for borrowing the funds. At the beginning of your loan's life the lion's share will be for interest and a minuscule amount for principal or equity. Conversely, at the end of your loan's life most of the payment will go to retiring principal while only a small amount will go toward interest.

For example, as the following chart shows, in the first year of a thirty-year, $100,000 loan, only 9% of your payment goes toward principal while 91% goes for interest (see Chart 19). In the fifteenth year, the middle of the loan's life, we find that 29 percent of the loan payment is for principal while the balance goes to interest. Finally, in the thirtieth year, just as the mortgage is paid off, virtually none of the loan payment is used for interest.

CHART 19

Division Between
Interest and Principal
Over 30 Years

Amount Borrowed = $100,000   Fixed Mortgage Rate = 8%

Year	Payment	=	Interest	+	Principal
1	$8805 (100%)		$7970 (91%)		$ 835 (9%)
2	$8805		$7900		$ 905
3	$8805		$7825		$ 980
4	$8805		$7744		$1061
5	$8805		$7656		$1149
6	$8805		$7561		$1245
7	$8805		$7457		$1348
8	$8805		$7345		$1460
9	$8805		$7224		$1581
10	$8805		$7093		$1712
11	$8805		$6951		$1854
12	$8805		$6797		$2008
13	$8805		$6630		$2175
14	$8805		$6450		$2355
15	$8805 (100%)		$6254 (71%)		$2551 (29%)
16	$8805		$6043		$2762

Year	Payment	=	Interest	+	Principal
17	$8805		$5813		$2992
18	$8805		$5565		$3240
19	$8805		$5296		$3509
20	$8805		$5005		$3800
21	$8805		$4690		$4116
22	$8805		$4348		$4457
23	$8805		$3978		$4827
24	$8805		$3577		$5228
25	$8805		$3143		$5662
26	$8805		$2673		$6132
27	$8805		$2165		$6641
28	$8805		$1613		$7192
29	$8805		$1016		$7789
30	$8805 (100%)		$ 370 (4%)		$8435 (96%)

The larger your down payment, the less money you need to borrow. And, accordingly, the less money you need to borrow, the less you'll have to pay in monthly mortgage installments.

Typically, the down payment must be at least 20 percent of the purchase price of the home. With a little legwork, you can find banks that will lend 90 percent, i.e., allowing you to put down 10 percent. In some parts of the country you can even find lenders willing to make a loan with only 5 percent down. Usually, young people are rich in income but poor in assets, so the mortgage payments are more affordable than the down payment.

Generally, lenders require mortgage payments to eat up no more than 30 to 35 percent of the gross income of the borrower. The information you provide on your mortgage application is used to determine your fixed costs, e.g., taxes, already outstanding loans, and other obligations. Put yourself in the lender's shoes for a moment. Their job is to make sure that once they lend you the money, you'll pay them back.

You're probably already worried about money. You don't think you have enough. I say you probably do. Maybe not today, but certainly tomorrow.

You Don't Have the Money for a Down Payment

We've already established how to determine how much you need and how to save up. You may not have the money today, but you can certainly have it tomorrow. You just need to adopt the mind-set that saving money to buy a house is what you want to do. How much money can you come up with? Can you borrow from your parents? (Specifics on this topic follow.) How much can you tap in employee savings plans? How much do you have in insurance? This all adds up. If you were to require a big chunk of cash tomorrow, you could probably do a lot better than you think —if you tap all your available resources. And that's what you'll have to do. After all, buying a house is your goal.

If you don't have enough for a down payment, you should turn back to your roots. Your parents might turn out to be a source of financing. In fact, for first-time home buyers, a helping hand from the family is usually critical. You needn't turn to your parents for a handout, though. The deal you make with your parents to borrow money can prove profitable for them as well.

Your particular situation will determine how you might want to structure such a deal. If you've got enough money, but not the credit history, your parents can co-sign on your loan. This would not obligate them to make monthly payments. However, if you fail to make a payment, they would then become liable. Assuming you have enough for the down payment, but cannot afford the monthly payments, another idea would be for your parents to help out with the monthly payments. A variant on this theme would be for your parents to make part or all of the down payment.

Besides enjoying the gift of giving, there are two financially sound reasons for parents to supply you with funds. First, they're not invincible. Someday they will, I'm sorry to say, pass away. If they give you the money now, up to $20,000 per year is exempt from taxation as a gift. Second, they could become your partner and share in the equity of your home.

Here are some examples of partnerships you could arrange with your parents. Your parents put up 50 percent of the down payment and make 50 percent of the mortgage payments. You split the tax benefits 50/50 and, when you finally sell the house, you split the capital gain 50/50. Alternatively, let's say you can afford the mortgage payments but don't have the money for a down payment. Your parents' share in the equity is the portion of the capital gain to which they are entitled. That is, at the beginning of the mortgage your parents make the down payment and thus put up 100 percent of the equity. But over time, through your mortgage payments, you add to the value of the equity, your share grows, and theirs diminishes. Let's assume you purchase a $100,000 condo and finance it with a fixed interest rate of 10 percent to be paid back over thirty years. Chart 20 depicts changes in your share of the equity versus your parents' over the first ten years:

CHART 20

	Financial Structure: You and Your Parents, Inc. 505 Main Street				
Year	Parents' Equity	+	Your Equity	=	Total Equity
Beginning	$10,000 (100%)		0 (0%)		$10,000
1	$10,000 (95%)		547 (5%)		$10,547
2	$10,000 (90%)		$1,149 (10%)		$11,149
3	$10,000 (85%)		$1,811 (15%)		$11,811
4	$10,000 (80%)		$2,539 (20%)		$12,539
5	$10,000 (75%)		$3,340 (25%)		$13,340
6	$10,000 (70%)		$4,221 (30%)		$14,421
7	$10,000 (66%)		$5,191 (34%)		$15,191
8	$10,000 (62%)		$6,257 (38%)		$16,257
9	$10,000 (57%)		$7,430 (43%)		$17,430
10	$10,000 (53%)		$8,720 (47%)		$18,720

You can see, with this arrangement, that your share of the equity increases over time. Sometime during the eleventh year your share exceeds 50 percent and your parents' dips below 50 percent. This investment holds out the promise of a worthy return for your parents.

Assume housing prices increase 5 percent per year. Accordingly, the place you buy for $100,000 will have a value on the marketplace of $105,000 next year. In two years it will be valued at $110,250 and so on. At the end of the first year your palace has appreciated by $5,000. If you were to sell it, you'd gain $5,000 on your investment. Because of the equity-sharing arrangement you've entered into, you'd have to give 95 percent of the gain to your partners while you'd keep 5 percent. You'd earn $250 while your parents would get $4,750.

This isn't a bad deal for them. They put up $10,000 and, one year later, they make $4,750. That's a 47.5 percent return. In the second year your home is now worth $110,250. If you sold then, the gain would equal $10,250. At that point your share of the equity would amount to 10 percent while they would be entitled to 90 percent. Accordingly, their gain would be 90 percent of that amount, or $9,225. They would earn 92 percent on their $10,000 investment. You, on the same hand, would be entitled to $1,025. Through making the monthly payments, your investment in the house amounts to $1,149. Your gain, in percentage terms, is the same, 92 percent. Because of the terms of the agreement, you both earn the same amount on your relative investment.

This is but one example of a way you can finance your house. When you put your mind to it you can devise many ways to finance purchasing a house or condo. Another way was highlighted at the beginning of Chapter 7. Chris financed his apartment by seeking out a partner, his best friend. Chris had to borrow a little from his mother, although most of the money came from his own savings. His partner, Jim, didn't have any money so he arranged with Chris to buy only 35 percent of the condo.

There are many sources of mortgage money. You can find a partner or you can find a lender. The government may be your banker if you're a veteran. Some institutions, specifically called "mortgage bankers" in newspaper advertisements, lend only for real estate. Another source of financing, which grew in importance in the early 1980s during the period of sky-high interest rates, was the seller. Because interest rates were so high, monthly mortgage payments were accordingly quite steep. As a consequence, only those with the highest incomes were being approved by banks. Sellers—stymied by their inability to sell their houses—often agreed to make secondary loans to the purchasers of their houses.

How Much House Can You Afford?

Now we get down to the nitty-gritty. We'll look at mortgages, evaluate lenders, and then zero in on how much you can afford.

In the planning section we determined how much you have in liquid and available assets. Glance back to that number. Subtract $1,000 from it. This is how much money you have to buy a co-op or house. I assume that $1,000 is enough in rainy-day savings. If that's not enough, then add to it. I do believe the minimum you should have in savings is $1,000.

Although you won't pay for the services of your real estate broker (the seller pays those costs, which are usually 6 percent of the purchase price), there are many other costs associated with buying a house. Local customs are different throughout the country and you may end up paying some or all of the charges listed below. However, more than likely, you'll be faced with the following charges.

You'll have to pay an application fee, which is usually nonrefundable. The origination fee is next in line. This is how much the bank will charge you to initiate the loan. This fee can also be referred to as "points" (percentage points). The bank or mortgage lender charges a percentage of the loan. For example, if you plan to borrow $100,000, and the bank charges 2 points, you will have to pay $2,000 (or 2 percent of 100,000) for the bank to process the loan.

Before the bank will make a loan to you, they'll require what is called a "title search." Typically, you pay for the bank to complete the search for you. This is done to ensure that the title to the property is free of any encumbrances. This confirms that the previous owners of the property did not promise the property to guarantee another loan. You'll also pay for title insurance, which guarantees the work of the title search. You also have to pay for the bank's appraisal of the property and the bank's attorneys.

As you search for a mortgage to buy—and you are *buying* a mortgage—make a list of estimated closing costs and interest charges. This will help you sort out the best deal. You're looking for a dependable, trustworthy lender, one that will complete the processing for your mortgage application in a reasonable amount of time. If you look through the weekend home advertisement section of your newspaper, you'll find extensive advertisements for banks and mortgage companies willing to give you a loan. Shop around. The interest rates and lengths of loans, fees, and charges vary extensively. (I can't argue strongly enough how important it is for you to shop around for the best mortgage deal you can find. As I wrote this book I was in the process of buying a condominium as an investment and spoke with twenty-five mortgage lenders. The best deal I found saved me more than $5,000 over the average deal offered by some of the largest banks.)

Mortgage Shopping

Once you compile all the data about prices, rates, and terms, there are two ways to compare deals. The first, called the "APR method," is simple, yet it will not prove as valuable as the more complicated method detailed below. Whenever you see a mortgage rate quoted, you'll usually see a second interest rate adjacent to it, in the same typeface, that says, "APR," annual percentage rate. The banks calculate their processing fees and interest charges over thirty years and determine the annual rate. You can use this number to compare with the rates and terms of other mortgages. This is a fine method if you plan to stay in your house for thirty years. Very, very few people—especially people at the beginning of their careers (e.g., you)—stay in their first house long enough to pay off the mortgage.

Here's a more appropriate, though more difficult, way. This method makes more realistic assumptions than the APR method.

First, estimate how long you're going to stay in this home. Nationally, the tenure averages twelve years. A young person or couple is more likely to stay less than five years. I recommend that first-time home buyers assume they'll remain in the house five years.

Second, isolate those costs associated with each bank. For example, you would not include real estate taxes on this list because you have to pay the same real estate taxes regardless of the bank from which you buy your mortgage.

List all the closing costs that you pay to the bank. Next, determine the yearly mortgage cost for each of the first five years. For fixed-rate mortgages, simply use the same value every year.

For adjustable-rate mortgages, assume the worst case for the direction of interest rates. That is, assume that the adjustment will rise the maximum amount allowed during every repricing period. For example, if your initial interest rate is 7 percent on a six-month adjustable-rate mortgage and your contract allows the interest rate to increase no more than 1 percent every repricing period, then assume your rate will jump 1 percent each period. First to 8 percent. Then to 9 percent. Then to 10 percent. Most adjustable-rate loans have ceilings; that is, contractually they cannot rise above a certain level.

A word of caution about adjustable-rate mortgages is required. Often banks will offer an introductory, first-year rate. After the first year the rate reverts to a higher rate that is more in line with other adjustable-rate mortgage interest rates. I have often found that even salespeople for the banks are not aware that the first year's rate is a special rate. A clear sign that the first year's rate is special is if it is significantly below the mortgage rates charged on similar mortgages (i.e., same adjustment period and same loan length) by several other lenders.

If you want to compare costs a full example of the analysis is described below. The final step is to discount the costs you pay in the future back to their present value. You'll remember from our earlier discussion that money has a time value. Money today is more valuable than the same amount in five years. You'd rather have it today than in five years. Hence, a cost you'll bear in five years is less important to you today than a cost you pay today.

You must take this into account when you compare costs. That's why it's important to take a stab at how long you'll be in this house.

For simplicity's sake, I have assumed a discount rate of 6 percent. It's important that discounting be done so as to compare apples to apples. To discount, simply divide by the factors I've included on Chart 21.

CHART 21

Calculating the Cost of a Mortgage

$$\text{Total } \$\underline{\quad} = \frac{\text{Closing Costs}}{1.00} + \frac{\text{Year 1}}{1.06^1} + \frac{\text{Year 2}}{1.06^2} + \frac{\text{Year 3}}{1.06^3} + \frac{\text{Year 4}}{1.06^4} + \frac{\text{Year 5}}{1.06^5}$$

I called up two New York City banks—the Big Bank and the Small S & L—to garner some mortgage cost information over the telephone. I compared the costs of a fixed-rate mortgage the Big Bank offered versus those of a three-year adjustable mortgage from the Small S & L. Let's assume you buy a $100,000 condo for which you put down 20 percent of the total purchase price, or $20,000. That means you're financing 80 percent. This is called an 80 percent loan, referring to the loan-to-value percentage. The Big Bank quoted a fixed rate of 11 percent while the Small S & L quoted a 9.12 percent rate on its three-year adjustable-rate loan. The closing costs were quoted to me over the phone as follows (see Chart 22):

CHART 22

	Comparing Two Banks' Mortgage Offerings	
	The Big Bank	The Small S & L
Points	2.5 Points or $2500	2 Points or $2000
Appraisal	$200	$250
Bank Lawyers	$295	$375
Title Search	$ 32	$100
Recording	$ 54	$ 28
Total Closing Costs	$3,081	$2,753

For the the Big Bank $100,000 fixed-payment loan, the monthly payments are $952, or $11,428 annually. On the Small S & L's three-year adjustable loan, the monthly payments are $823, or $9,872 annually. At the end of the third year of the loan, we assume that interest rates hike upward. The terms of the loan allow a maximum adjustment of three percentage points. Accordingly, we assume that the rate moves from 9.125 to 12.125 percent for the fourth and fifth years of the loan.

Consequently, the monthly payments move up to $1,038, or $12,575 annually. To compare all these apples and oranges we need to discount them back to the present, dividing by the factors from the previous table (see Chart 23). Now the final calculation is to add up the present value of mortgage payments plus the closing costs to determine which is the better deal (see Chart 24):

CHART 23

Comparing the Two Deals

| Year 1 | Year 2 | Year 3 | Year 4 | Year 5 |

The Big Bank

Actual Costs

$11,428 $11,428 $11,428 $11,428 $11,428

Present Value

$48,139 = $10,781 + $10,171 + $9,595 + $9,052 + $8,540

The Small S & L

Actual Costs

$9,872 $9,872 $9,872 $12,575 $12,575

Present Value

$45,745 = $9,313 + $8,786 + $8,289 + $9,960 + $9,397

CHART 24

	The Big Bank	The Small S & L
Closing Costs	$3,081	$2,753
Mortgage Payments, Present Value	$48,139	$45,745
Total	$51,220	$48,498

This evaluation shows that, financially speaking, it's better to buy a mortgage at the Small S & L. Of course there are several other factors that go into the calculation, such as turnaround time, how long it will take to process your application. And if you assume that you'll stay in your house or condo longer than five years and that interest rates are going to continue moving up, then the calculation results tilt more in favor of the Big Bank.

The general idea of comparing mortgage costs is to find out all the closing costs and then add those to the cost of the mortgage during the first five years of the mortgage's life. Now let's go to the fun stuff.

Financial Benefits from Real Estate

I've touched on the financial benefits derived from investing in a palace of your own and now I plan to lay these out more definitively. There are three and one half financial benefits that arise from investing in real estate over other forms of investments.

The first benefit is simply stated by *Money* magazine: "There is scarcely another product that you can buy, use, and then sell for more than you paid for it."* In other words, you nearly get to live for free.

The second benefit is leverage. Leverage refers to the degree of risk you assume relative to the amount of money you put up. For example, if you buy a $100,000 house with a $10,000 down payment, you're leveraged 10 to 1. You own $10 in assets for every $1 you invest. Nowhere else in the investing world can you assume such a high degree of leverage with such a low-risk investment.

Finally, there are the tax benefits as Uncle Sam steps in. The fathers of the country decided many years ago that home ownership was a good thing for the functioning of society. They decided to help out the good people of this country. They faced a choice: They could buy homes for everyone or they could provide tax incentives to foster home ownership over other forms of investments. The latter translated is mortgage-interest deduction.

Uncle Sam allows you to deduct your mortgage payments from your gross salary and other sources of income. If you pay mortgage payments based on a 10 percent interest before taxes, your actual after-tax interest cost will always be less. Say you're in a 28 percent tax bracket, a 10 percent before-tax interest cost drops down to 7.2 percent. If you're in a combined 35 percent tax bracket, your after-tax interest payment amounts to 6.5 percent. Remember, your effective tax bracket includes the state and local taxes you pay as well as the federal taxes.

* "Your Home," *Money Guide: Your Home,* (New York: Time Inc.), p. 9.

The "half" of the three and a half benefits of investing in real estate comes from equity. Equity refers to your share of ownership in the building. All things considered, equity is a good thing. You can borrow against your equity. Rarely, though, will you cash in your equity when you sell your house by buying a less expensive house. When you work up your financial assets your equity will go a long way to making you feel better off. And you get equity when you own. Nevertheless, the growth in equity is just a side benefit you get when you own rather than a distinct, sought-after benefit.

Grow Your Equity

There are three ways that your equity—your investment in your house—increases: one is by your being smart, the second is a natural result of the mortgage payment structure, and the third is by pursuing a financially unsound course of action.

Real estate prices are still increasing, not as fast as they did several years ago, but nevertheless they are still going up. Your equity stake increases without so much as your having to lift a finger. If you put $10,000 down on a $100,000 house and a year later it is worth $110,000, it means your equity has increased from $10,000 to $20,000. (In reality, your equity position will be slightly greater because a piddling amount of your total mortgage payment at the beginning goes toward paying off the principal to the bank.) By buying a house that appreciates in value at least as fast as the general market, you've done your job.

The second way your equity increases is a natural function of the mortgage payment structure. As we discussed before, each month a portion of your monthly payments goes toward interest, with the rest going toward paying the outstanding principal. At the beginning of your mortgage's life the bulk of your payment is slated for interest coverage. As your mortgage ages you pay more in principal and less in interest.

The third way to increase your equity is to pay off your mortgage faster than you have to. I believe this is an ill-advised practice from an investment point of view. Every month you owe your mortgage payment. The bank kindly tells you how much of your payment is scheduled for interest coverage and how much will go toward increasing your equity. If you double the principal you pay each month, you would pay off your thirty-year mortgage in fifteen years. By increasing the money you have sitting in your house, you are establishing a savings account called "My House." The market value of your house will not change at all because you're paying your mortgage off faster. In other words, the rate of return on increasing your principal payments is zero. That's right, zip. This is why I don't advise paying off your mortgage at an accelerated rate.

If you want to pay off your thirty-year mortgage in fifteen years, a far better way would be to establish a money market account and put that additional money into this account. By this method, in fact, you'd pay it off faster than fifteen years—you'd have the accumulated interest to pay off the principal.

Investing In Real Estate

Walk into any business section of any bookstore and chances are you will find many books on investing in real estate: *How I Turned $1,000 into Five Million in Real Estate In My Spare Time,* a classic. *Nothing Down,* a best-seller. *How You Can Become Financially Independent by Investing in Real Estate.* (In the early 1980s real estate investment books became a U.S. cottage industry.)

By and large, a house that is good for living in is also a house that is a good investment. Investing in real estate—strictly for profit—as opposed to buying a house or condo for you and your loved ones has some dramatic pluses. (There are some minuses as well.)

The first positive aspect is leverage. I've talked at length about the leverage involved in buying yourself a house: buying a $100,000 asset for $10,000 down with minimal risk for loss. You can't do that in the stock market. As you'll see in the appendix to the next chapter, you can be as highly leveraged, if not more so, with stock options. However, with these options, your potential for a total loss is infinitely greater than in real estate.

The second major benefit from real estate investment stems from something accountants call the "noncash charge." That's depreciation. When you own your own home and you live in same, you cannot depreciate it. However, the minute you move out of your home and a renter moves in, you can depreciate it.

Depreciation won't cost you a cent. Instead, it is a charge against your income from the property that you do not have to pay. Let's say you own a piece of property where the renters just cover your mortgage interest charges and any incidental upkeep expenses you may have. On a cash-flow basis, you just break even. All the rental income goes right back out again for debt service, taxes, and the upkeep.

It comes time to do your taxes and you collect your receipts. You look in your checkbook and find that your cash expenses are just covered by your rental income. Now—your rental real estate depreciated over the year. (For tax purposes you are not allowed to depreciate the property, only the structure on the property.) That is, on paper you have an additional expense that didn't cost you any money. You deduct that from your position at the end of the year and you show a loss. You can deduct this loss from your gross income in calculating your net taxable income. The value of the deduction is simply your tax bracket multiplied by the amount of the loss. Thus, by losing money on paper, but not out of your pocket, you reduce your taxes—on paper and out of your pocket.*

Real estate investment is not nearly as liquid as stocks. You can't get out of the investment with just a phone call to your broker. (Despite what the ads may say.) Second, managing rental property requires work. You have to find tenants. You have to maintain the building. More than likely, but not always, you'll have to hold the property for a long time before you see any substantial gain. That wasn't the case with the Kaangolds and their first rental real estate purchase.

---

* The taxation rules on real estate investment have changed and this tax advantage outlined here may not apply, depending on your income level.

$100,000 in a Year

James Kaangold and his wife, Judy, both age twenty-nine, recently had their first child and purchased their second rental income property. They took a slightly different tack to real estate investing than is usual.

James: While we were renting, we bought a house in the neighborhood that we eventually wanted to settle in. It's a three-bedroom, two-bath, two-story house in a pleasant suburb of Connecticut. It has a deep backyard and was built in 1929. Instead of buying a place that we were going to live in, we bought a place that we really couldn't afford to live in. We could afford to buy it and rent it out. Hopefully, we'll be able to live in it someday.

Me: How do you figure?

James: The payments were originally $1,400 per month. We couldn't afford that. The place was on the market for $160,000. For a 10 percent-down loan, we would have had to pay additional insurance and survey costs for the bank. I figured it made more sense to put down 20 percent. My wife and I had saved up around $18,000. To make the $32,000 down payment, I borrowed $5,000 through an "executive" unsecured credit line from my bank and $15,000 from my parents.

Me: What kind of mortgage loan did you take out?

James: We took out a one-year adjustable-rate loan at 10 1/2 percent that was 2 1/4 percent over one-year Treasury bonds.

Me: How much were your monthly payments?

James: All told, the monthly expenses amounted to $1,400. Now there was no way that Judy and I could afford that. However, what we did was to rent out the place for $1,200 per month. At that rate we were running a loss of $200 per month, or $2,400 per year. But, and here's the reason it makes sense, the tax savings from depreciation outweighed the cash-flow loss. Here, look [see Chart 25]:

CHART 25

| | James's and Judy's Two Sets of Books Monthly Results | |
	Cash Flow	Tax Books
Rental Income	$1,200	$1,200
Interest Expense and Upkeep	−$1,400	−$1,400
Total Before Taxes	−$200	−$200
Depreciation		−$740
Total Loss w/ Depreciation		−$940
Tax Reduction: 28% Bracket [$940 × 28%]	+$263	
Total Cash Flow	$ 63	

To explain James's calculations, you have to carry two sets of books. This is perfectly legal and, in fact, dictated by the government's conventions. Each month James's tenants pay $1,200. James is required to send the bank $1,400. He's short $200 per month.

The government in effect says, "James and Judy, we appreciate risk-taking and entrepreneurship. We understand that businesses can sometimes be a losing proposition. So, here's what we'll do: If you incur a loss in your business, you can deduct that loss from your gross income."

The young couple is out $200 per month. However, at the end of the year, when they calculate how well their business did, they add in depreciation. The depreciation magnifies the loss. This loss is applied against their gross income. The value of the tax deduction is simply their tax bracket multiplied by the business loss: Et voilà, the marginal business becomes a winning proposition.

In the second year of the business the interest charges dropped to $1,200 because of the downward adjustment in his mortgage interest rate. At the same time they raised the rent by $50. Hence, now they enjoy a positive cash flow of $50 per month, even before considering the tax benefits.

Me: What about tenants?
James: Originally we thought we could handle renting it out ourselves. However, after several credit-lousy candidates came by, we turned to a broker. The broker saved us many headaches. We had to pay the broker one month's rent to find us tenants. But the tenants have worked out.
Me: You're still renting. Why didn't you buy your own place and live in it originally?
James: I knew that I wanted to live in the neighborhood that we chose. However, I couldn't really afford to live there. We bought this place that we assumed would keep escalating in price at the same rate as the rest of the neighborhood. I figured that eventually my salary would permit me to afford the payments.
Me: What do you estimate the value is today, a year after you bought it?
James: $260,000.
Me: That means you made $100,000 in a year's time on an investment of $32,000, or 312.5 percent.
James: Real estate has been very, very good to me.

Real estate has many advantages, which we've discussed in this chapter. Yet it isn't the only place to invest. Indeed, because of the large capital requirements and time commitments required in real estate, the stock and bond market may better fit your needs today. We turn to that subject.

SECTION

D | INVEST

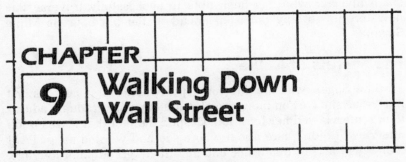

CHAPTER 9 Walking Down Wall Street

Stocks and Bonds

On glancing through the business pages of any newspaper, you'll find yesterday's closing quotes from the securities markets. You'll find quotes from the New York Stock Exchange, the American Stock Exchange, and the National Over-the-Counter (OTC) market, as well as some locally traded OTC's. There are 30,000 stock investment opportunities in print before your eyes. And we haven't even mentioned the bond market yet. Or options. What about pork bellies or frozen-orange-juice futures? And then there are permutations of all these securities, the mutual funds and index options and options on futures. Money market funds? Tax-exempts? Junk bonds?

Financial deregulation and the easing of restrictions by the Securities and Exchange Commission (SEC) have opened up whole new worlds of investing opportunities. *Forbes* magazine claims that "along with the changes wrought by the internalization of the world's economy and improvements in communications technology, the markets have become unusually volatile, jumpy, wide-swinging. Bonds move sharply, the foreign exchange market undergoes lightning-fast shifts in currency strengths and weaknesses, and commodities prices lurch from highs to lows."*

* Susan Lee, "What's with the Casino Society?" *Forbes* (New York: Forbes, Inc. September 22, 1986), p. 150.

Meantime, the difficulties of correctly gauging an appropriate investment for small investors have increased manifold. One such small investor who has been able to successfully traverse this new terrain, to stay one step ahead of the big boys, is Millie Sagan.

The Secrets of Millie

Millie Sagan was looking for a job when I first met her. At thirty-one she was on the verge of completing her graduate education. I interviewed her for a job. Despite the fact that it was a job interview, I didn't care about where she had worked as a CPA, I didn't give a whit about her undergraduate grade-point average, and I wasn't interested in what she wanted to be doing in five years. What piqued my curiosity was something printed in big, bold capital letters on her resume. It read, "STOCK MARKET RESULTS: Managed my personal investment portfolio, currently valued in excess of $60,000."

"You did what?" I asked.

"A few years ago" she responded, "while I was still working, I invested in my company's employee savings plan. After I'd accumulated several thousand dollars, I decided I could do better [than the fund managers] and I wanted to play the market."

"You did fairly well," I said.

"Yes, I have," she agreed.

"What's your secret?" I asked.

"I have three" was her reply.

"Will you tell me?"

"Sure," she said, "this is a job interview. First, I don't buy at the top. In other words, I look for undervalued situations. For instance, several years ago I bought Bank of America. The company had reported depressed earnings and its stock price tumbled. But I knew that the country's second largest bank wasn't about to collapse, and if it looked like it was about to collapse, the Feds would step in to rescue it. They weren't about to let a bank of that magnitude go under. I was right. It doubled in value several months later and I sold out my position. I made $8,000 on that one."

"Good gosh!" I exclaimed.

"Second, I buy only New York Stock Exchange stocks. I figure that stocks on the Big Board are so heavily traded that I'll never have problems moving a stock at a specific price. And the institutions are so heavily involved in these stocks that they literally will support them."

I said to her, "That's a very different outlook than most people have. Most advisers will tell you to stay away from such stocks precisely because when the big institutions make a move, a small investor could get trampled. And third?"

"I know that when I buy a stock," she said strongly, "it's going to go down."

"How's that?" I questioned.

"It's impossible to buy at the bottom," she acknowledged. "As much as I try to seek out undervalued situations, I know that I can't pick the absolute bottom. So when I buy a stock I just assume it's going to keep going down. That way I'm not upset when it goes down. Plus, if I've done my homework right, it's not going to remain that way for long."

"But how do you," I probed, "know when to get out of a loser?"

Her smug reply was, "In my five years in the market, I've never lost on one stock."

"That's pretty lucky," I said. "Do you set sell limits? That is, do you say if it goes down to X, then sell, or if it goes up to Y, then sell?"

"No, I see how the market's doing and take that into consideration."

"I see," I concluded.

In this chapter we'll examine the basic strategies of security investment. We'll look at what a stock actually is and where its price comes from. We'll also examine bonds. An underlying aim, as well, is to gain an understanding of the mechanics of securities trading, such as reading the securities tables, finding a broker, and learning the vocabulary. Ninety-five percent of the securities business, of playing the game, is just speaking the right language. Because option contracts are playing a greater and greater role in the investment world, I have included a section on them in the appendix for this chapter. I believe it is important to understand what they are, how they work, and how you can make and lose money with option contracts. However, as you'll see in the appendix, most people lose when playing options, so it is not advisable to include them in your financial strategy.

Being a smart investor doesn't require sleuthing out the companies that are about to make big moves. It doesn't require poring over charts, annual reports, 10-K's (SEC-required documents), and other investment paraphernalia. You can hire people to perform those services for you. However, being a smart investor does require understanding the work performed by your investment advisers. It does require an understanding that a 30 to 100 percent return on investment has to be a risky investment. (See appendix on options for risky investments.) In fact, you can hire investment advisers who will take all the day-to-day worry away from you. You'll learn about them in the next chapter.

I do have a bias, which I should state up front. Just as in the movie *The Graduate* where, at the wedding party, a father whispers "plastics" into Dustin Hoffman's ear, that being the purported secret of financial success, I say "mutual funds." I devote the next chapter to an explanation of this bias and why I think that they're the right investment for people in our position. When you finish these two chapters you'll be able to walk down Wall Street with breezy confidence.

The Stock Market

The story of the Haloid Corporation is a legendary one. Chester Carlson was born in 1906 and later turned out an invention that today is called the most successful commercial product invention in history. An early investment of $10,000 in Mr. Carlson's company (which, by the way, was passed up by IBM in the 1950s) would have yielded many millions of dollars. Carlson's brainchild could reproduce documents. Haloid became Xerox—the mythical investment. "It could be the next Xerox"* is a quote I've heard more than a few times.

Your investment in Haloid could have been the next Xerox, but as financial planner Stan Cohen points out, "You bought Haloid in 1956 when xerography was only a dream in Dr. Carlson's mind. Three years later, your miracle stock was trading at a third of what you paid for it and you were yelling at your broker for sticking you with a dog. Sell, you told him, I'll take the tax loss."†

There's no doubt that picking the next Xerox at just the right time is a thorny issue. To understand how to pick the next Xerox, it's important to understand just what a stock represents. It's really very simple. It starts with someone who has a hot idea, an invention, a new service, or a product. Maybe he or she is yearning to drill an oil well or open a shopping mall, produce a film, or invent a telephone that doubles as a microwave oven.

The one common denominator across all these ideas is that without any money, they will go nowhere. The entrepreneur needs money—usually lots of it. He first looks to his own pocket. If it's not deep enough and his family isn't Du Pont, then he looks to his friends' pockets. After raising as much as he can through personal sources, he finally goes to the bank.

Mr. Three-Piece Suit Banker ushers the entrepreneur into his office. The coffee is poured and the conversation lasts just long enough for the banker to learn of the entrepreneur's lack of collateral. After talking with the banker, our entrepreneur learns that he can't borrow enough money to make a go of it. He then visits an investment banker (an investment banker is a deal maker who arranges financing). The investment banker has a bigger Wall Street office and fancier Brooks Brothers attire than the commercial banker. The two shake hands and sit down. The entrepreneur falls into the lost recesses of an old, overstuffed leather chair. The investment banker riffles his fingers, has his secretary hold all

---

* David Owen, "Copies in Seconds," *The Atlantic Monthly* (Boston: February 1986), pp. 65–72.

† Stanley J. Cohen and Robert Wool, *How to Survive on $50,000 to $150,000 a Year* (New York: Viking Penguin Books, 1984), pp. 120–121.

calls, weaves his fingers into a little tent on his old, oversized mahogany desk, stares off, and barks, "How much do you need?" Our entrepreneur stutters, stammers, backpedals, and then, in a moment of abandon, cries out a number with many zeros. The investment banker cryptically replies, "We'll have to think about financing this idea and get back to you."

After deciding affirmatively to back the entrepreneur, the investment banker has two basic ways of financing the company: issuing bonds—debt—or issuing stock—equity. With debt, the investment banker swaps corporate IOU's for money that eventually is repaid by the entrepreneur's company. With equity—which is never repaid—the investment banker trades shares denoting ownership for money.

If all goes well and the equity route is chosen, several months later, sometimes years later, a public issue of stock is brought to the market. It is called an "initial public offering," or IPO. The investment banker has arranged a syndicate of brokerage houses around the country to market this new security. The public buys claims of ownership in the firm. The investment banker hands over the money to the entrepreneur and collects a tidy fee for supervising the transaction.

During the initial public offering, the stock is sold directly to investors. However, if these first public investors want to sell their shares afterward, they must go to the public marketplace. In most instances, the security will trade in the Over-the-Counter (OTC) market. The OTC market refers to the process of trading shares among brokerage houses over the phone as opposed to on the floor of established exchanges. In the days before the Great Depression, banks routinely used to trade securities. To buy or sell a security, the investor could go to a bank and exchange the certificate *Over the Counter* of a bank—and thus the name Over-the-Counter. As the company grows it will eventually qualify to be listed on one of the exchanges. It is not required for securities above a certain size to trade on the exchange floor. It is more a sign of prestige, and it improves the ease of trading for the security.

If you look at a firm's balance sheet, you'll see a listing of assets and liabilities and stockholders equity. The assets must equal the firm's liabilities and equity. The liabilities of the firm are claims by the company's creditors and suppliers. If all the assets of the firm were sold off—or liquidated—tomorrow, all the debts would be paid off from the available assets. The remaining assets would then be distributed to the owners, the shareholders.

You'll often hear the term "book value." This refers to the value of ownership, on the books, held by the owners, the shareholders of the firm. Determining book value is simple—subtract the debt from the assets, and what's left over is the stockholders equity or book value. The per-share book value is the total stockholders equity divided by the number of shares.

Book value often bears little resemblance to market value, the price that shares sell for on the open market. Nine times out of ten, book value will be less than the market value. This gives rise to the question, Where does market value come from?

Why Such a Price?

"Buy undervalued situations," says Millie, along with countless others. Many stockbrokers, financial planners, and soothsayers will tell you likewise. Fine. That's just a corollary of the "Buy low, sell high" dictum.

The reason a stock, or any security for that matter, has a price in the first place is because that's the market value. The market is often seen as a faceless monolith that moves arbitrarily and ruthlessly. This isn't the case. The market *is* the millions of individual investors and institutions buying and selling. The collective wisdom of these millions of individuals—the marketplace—gives value to securities.

For example, on the day that I wrote this IBM closed at 150 7/8, or $150.88. I don't care what IBM's price was yesterday and what its price was a year ago. All I know is what I read in the paper today. And the gathered wisdom or stupidity of the marketplace —all the institutions, all the bank trust companies, all the mutual funds, all the employees of IBM, all the small investors, all of them—have decided that the value of one share of IBM at the closing bell was worth 150 7/8. Is it undervalued? Perhaps over-valued? Maybe it's just right?

Beauty is in the eye of the beholder. For everybody who thought that it was undervalued, there were an equal number who thought it was overvalued. When all the paper settled, when all the shouting was over on the corner of Broad and Wall streets at the New York Stock Exchange in New York City, when the tape finally shut down, the view was that 150 7/8 was the right price. That doesn't mean, of course, it won't change tomorrow. It's a new day. The world changes. Who knows? IBM might buy the federal government.

There are a million and one ways to explain and predict the future direction of a stock. For example, the holding company of United Airlines, Westin Hotels, and Hertz recently changed its name from UAL, Inc. to the Allegis Corporation. The president said that this made-up word sounded like *allegiance* and *aegis* (which means "protection"). What this had to do with running an airline, a rent-a-car agency, and a hotel chain escaped me, and I wasn't alone. One explanation for the change offered by a respected airline-security analyst and reported in *The New York Times* was, "I can understand their need for a new identity because they haven't done well in the stock market. . . . Maybe they think it [the name change] can help their stock."* Of course this is nonsense. If changing the name of the company to a heretofore nonexistent word alone could improve the stock price, companies would do this all the time. There are two ways to gauge a stock's future price that make more sense.

Dog and Pony

A stock's price depends in an offhand way on the effectiveness of the corporation's public relations efforts. The largest companies and many of the smaller ones have become quite good at staging dog-and-pony shows. These are extravaganzas whereby

* Steven Greenhouse, "Allegis? That's the Old UAL," *The New York Times*, February 19, 1987, p. D4.

the president and some of the top executives make presentations to security analysts across the country. Their aim is to generate excitement among individual, as well as institutional, investors. The general idea is that you won't get full price for your product—the stock, in this instance—unless everyone knows how good it is. And how do they know how good it is? Easy, you tell them. The purpose of these shows is to impress the analysts with the growth and earnings prospects for the company.

A typical annual report for a Fortune 500 firm costs in the tens of thousands of dollars. They're replete with four-color pictures and written by the most professional copywriters that money can buy. There's a reason corporations blow so much money on these things. The people who read them, by and large, are security analysts. What do you think the security analysts would think of a firm's prospects if the annual report was typed and mimeographed and devoid of photos?

This is the reality. Money—the kind with a capital M and many zeros—is spent impressing the people who invest billions of dollars. How much these publicity trimmings improve a security's market price, I don't know. You could postulate that because so many firms spend so much money on these kinds of activities, it must have a considerable effect.

The more serious explanation behind a stock's price relates to its anticipated future earnings and interest rates. If you own a share of stock, say, of Exxon, you have a tiny, tiny claim of ownership, a little piece of that company. As an owner, of course, you have a claim on the assets of the company, an obligation for the debts of the company, and a right to the earnings of the company. You have hired the board of directors of the firm to manage the company for you. Of course you couldn't show up on Exxon's doorstep in New York and say "I'm here—I want to cash in my share. Tell me where my oil well is." As an owner in the company, your share entitles you to receive dividends and to share in the future growth of the share price.

As the company prospers and shows a profit, it can pay out the money in dividends or plow the money back into its operations to promote future growth. Exxon in 1985 paid $3.61 in dividends on earnings per share of $5.83. Ergo, the firm retained $2.22 of its 1985 profits per share to fuel future growth:

1985 Per Share Results

Profit per Share	$5.83
− Dividend per Share	$3.61
= Retained Earning per Share	$2.22

On January 2, 1986, Exxon sold for $51.63 per share. If you bought, it would have entitled you to receive dividend payments and to sell the stock whenever you wanted, presumably at a higher amount. You'd sell if you thought the price was going to go down or if you thought the dividend payments plus any future price appreciation would be less than what you could earn elsewhere.

Let's make some assumptions. First, for a brief moment, let's assume that Exxon paid out all its earnings in dividends. That means you'd earn $5.83 on your $51.63 investment in 1986. That's an 11 percent return, 11.24%, to be exact. Not bad. Let's also assume that for the next twenty years the dividend payout remained constant at $5.83. At the end of the twenty years, let's assume that Exxon goes bust. After paying out all earnings, poor Exxon doesn't have anything left. The managers hadn't planned for any future growth by this strategy. Somewhere along about the twelfth year, they started to mortgage their properties to keep making dividend payments. The firm was really limping along in the eighteenth and nineteenth years. Finally, by the twentieth year, desks and buildings were sold, and eventually the gas stations were all gone. Exxon has ceased to exist. Your stock has absolutely no value.

A share doesn't entitle you to anything but more money in the future. It presents a stream of earnings either in dividend payments (as in the example we've constructed) or in some combination of dividend payments and capital gains. To calculate the real value of the share today, we would determine the present value of the twenty-year stream of earnings by discounting them at an appropriate interest rate. You'll recall discounting from the savings chapter, where we calculated how much you need to have today to achieve your goal tomorrow.

It's the same thing with stock prices. The question is, How much do you pay today for value in the future? That's why the analysts make a big deal about estimating next year's earnings. It's vital in the calculation of what today's stock price will/should be.

Let's go back to the real world. Nobody has a crystal ball. And Exxon isn't going to fold in twenty years. A share's price today reflects your view and other investors' views about future dividends and earnings gains. Most firms plow their earnings back into the business and pay out a small amount, if any, in dividends. You buy a stock today precisely because you think that its earnings per share are going to grow in the future. That earnings growth will fuel the stock price upward. The stock market is a forward-looking creature. It doesn't care about what happened yesterday—that's old news. The earnings outlook for the future is what counts.

Pee-Eee's and Other Hieroglyphics

The earnings per share reflect the theoretical yearly return on investment per share. Remember, as a shareholder you own a small claim on any earnings that the company enjoys.

The relationship between the earnings and the price is highly regarded and watched on Wall Street. The indicator is the price-to-earnings ratio. The price/earnings ratio, or P/E—pronounced Pee-Eee—is simply the current price of the share divided by the earnings over the most recent period. Usually the newspaper will print the price/earnings ratio as suggested by the previous year's or the previous quarter's earnings. A more relevant indicator is the current price divided by the estimated earnings over the next year. The stock market looks only to the future. However, to estimate earnings, you've got to get your crystal ball warmed up.

A more revealing way of thinking about the price/earnings ratio is to take its reciprocal—that is, instead of looking at a price/earnings ratio of 8.9 and saying "Hmm, looks good to me," you flip it on its head, 1/ 8.9, or .1123596, and say "Hmm, still looks good to me." This is the theoretical return on investment that you earn by investing in a particular company. For example, Exxon's P/E was 8.9. Dividing 1 by 8.9 results in the figure .1124, or 11.24 percent. We've seen this number before. It's your theoretical return on investment. The price of the stock will change and the earnings estimates for the coming year will change as well. Hence, the P/E will change frequently. As you contemplate an investment in Exxon today, the inverse of the P/E tells you how the market gauges the current prospects for Exxon.

The P/E for one company is often compared with that of another company in the same industry group. For instance, in the above example it is said that it will cost you $8.90 (in stock price) to earn $1.00 (in earnings). This number is compared with others in the same industry to determine the value of this choice. The relation between price and earnings is called the multiple.

A typical stock quote in the newspaper will look as follows:

	Sales	P/E	Yield	Open	High	Low	Close	Change
Exxon	736	89	6%	$52^1/4$	$52^1/4$	$51^3/8$	$51^5/8$	$-5/8$

Sales figures, always quoted in thousands, tell you how many shares traded hands on the previous day. The "P/E" tells you what the current price is, divided by the earnings for the previous year or for the previous quarter annualized. The "Yield" refers to dividend yield. It is calculated by dividing the most recent year dividend payout by the current price of the stock. The "Open" column refers to what the stock opened at; the "High" and "Low" refer to the highs and lows of the day; and the "Close" tells you the price of the last transaction of the day.

Bonds

Much of the same activity—guessing, outguessing, undervaluing, overvaluing—goes on in the bond market as well. The nature of the beast isn't as tricky, however, at least on the face of it.

A bond is nothing more than a loan. I make a loan, expecting you to return it next year. It's called a loan or a note. I give Exxon

$1,000 today and expect them to give it back to me in twenty years. It becomes a bond. It's still a loan, a note, paper, or a bond. These terms all involve the same thing: lending money.

The three relevant criteria for appraising a bond's value are its price today, its coupons, and its expiration date. Most bonds come in denominations of $1,000. If you buy a bond at $1,000, it is said to be priced at "par." If you pay more than that, you're paying a premium, while if you pay less, you're buying at a discount. Its coupons are the amount of interest paid each period, typically semiannually.

When I wrote this, certain Exxon bonds, the "Exxon11s87" bond, were being sold at 102¼, or $102.25 with one year to maturity. Bonds are quoted in multiples of $100, even though you have to pay ten times as much to buy one. This means an Exxon bond with a stated interest rate of 11 percent (the number following the name) that paid its coupons semiannually (that's what the "s" means) would cost you $1,022.50 ($102.25 × 10) to buy. Since the bond paid 11 percent, or $110, semiannually, you would receive two checks from Exxon, one at mid-year for $55 and the other $55 at the end of the year. Also, at the end of 1987, at maturity, Exxon returns the initial capital, the $1,000, lent in the first place.

Let's assume for a moment that you hold the bond until it matures. Hence, you face no risk about your stream of payments, which will be $55 and $1,055. If we make the simplifying assumption that you receive both coupon payments simultaneously with the $1,000 principal repayment, that is, you get all $1,110 at one time, the effective rate of return on your investment is 8.56 percent:

$$\frac{\text{Return}}{\text{Cost}} = \frac{\$1,000 + \$55 + \$55}{\$1,022} = (1 + 8.56\%)$$

Even though the stated interest rate is 11 percent—what it says on the face of the bond certificate—you have to pay more than $1,000 to buy the bond. Accordingly, your effective yield is lower. If you had paid only $1,000 to buy the bond, your effective yield would have been 11 percent, the coupon rate. (In reality you get the first payment, $55, six months earlier than the second coupon payment and the principal repayment. Hence, you could turn around and invest that $55 for six months. If you were to do this, your effective return on investment from buying the bond would be slightly higher, 8.63 percent.)

Let's run through another example. The "Exxon6s97" bonds are selling for 75 1/8, or $721.25, per bond. Again, this means you'll receive semiannual payments amounting to $30 each for this bond, which comes due in 1997. The coupon rate is 6 percent, and since the market yield for similar interest is higher than 6 percent, you'll pay less than $1,000 for this bond. That is, it has to cost you less to buy the bond than it would if interest rates were 6 percent to induce you to buy the bond. You'll pay only $751.25 to buy this bond. The effective yield on this investment is 10.57 percent.

This is a critical principle of bond math: As the price goes up, the effective interest rate you'll earn goes down. The converse holds true as well: As the bond's price drops, the effective interest rate goes up.

You'll earn 10.57 percent if you hold this bond to maturity in 1997. If you sell before expiration, the future market price of the bond when you sell becomes important. This is because you are no longer assured of receiving $1,000 in nineteen years. The price of the bond is based on:

1. The supply and demand for similar bonds.
2. The rate of return on risk-free Treasury bills.
3. The safety rating given to it by bond-rating services.
4. The market's view about the future of the company and its ability to pay debts.
5. Perceptions about the U.S. Treasury's fiscal and the Fed's monetary actions.
6. The future direction of the economy.
7. The borrowing habits of major U.S. trade partners, such as the Japanese.

I hope to have established two things through this lengthy discourse on the mathematics of stock and bond pricing: that it's a complicated matter intricately affected by prevailing market interest rates, and if you can correctly forecast the direction of interest rates, you'll be ahead of the game.

Which Way Are Interest Rates Headed?

You can always open the newspaper and find an article about what the stock and bond markets did on the prior day or the prior week. Often the writer will claim that the markets moved in a certain direction—either up or down (it usually doesn't matter)—and explain that it was a reaction to (a) the Fed's recent moves, (b) a speech made by the chairman of the Fed, (c) some offhand comment that the President made. Let's look at what the Fed does.

The Federal Reserve Bank is the nation's bank. The people who sit on the Federal Reserve Board can loosely influence interest rates. The key word here is *loosely*. The Fed does not control the nation's money supply, contrary to popular belief. The economy—the banks, the investors, the employees, foreign governments' state banks—does that.

The Fed used to try to control interest rates by changing the discount rate, the interest rates charged to banks for lending them money. At the end of the 1970s, with inflation rampant, the Fed kept pushing up the discount rates in an attempt to choke off inflation. The thinking went as follows: If money became so expensive, businesses and consumers would quit borrowing, the economy would cool off, and inflation would settle into quietude. That didn't happen. Instead, by increasing the cost of money, the cost of everything else started to go up even more. People borrowed as much as they could because they knew that they'd be paying off that debt with cheaper dollars. That's what inflation's all about.

The Fed said, "Okay, we give up. We can't control inflation by trying to change interest rates . . . it's the growth in the money supply that drives inflation," and so they began to try to influence the money supply. One view holds that money, like any other commodity, is subject to the effects of supply and demand. If the

supply exceeds demand, the price goes down. That is, the value of
the dollar decreases. As the money supply grows larger and
larger, faster than the economy is growing, the value of the dollar
diminishes. That's inflation. The Fed then said, "We're going to
keep our eye on the growth rate of the money supply. That way
we'll be able to check inflation."

Funny thing, though: They found that the money supply is determined by the banks and by how quickly people spend money and
by the federal government's borrowings from the public. The
question that then arose was, What the heck is money, anyway?
If a bank authorizes a line of credit—which can be turned into
cash as quickly as you can say "Visa"—should that be counted as
money? Is money that you keep in an equity mutual fund as your
savings considered money or is that stock? There are countless
other examples of securities that act much like money. One
thing's for certain, though, money ain't what it used to be.

The Fed's attempt to control the money supply had a peculiar
effect, one that was largely unforeseen. Interest rates moved not
so much because of the supply and demand for credit but because
of the expectations about what the Federal Reserve Board was
planning next. The Federal Reserve Board chairman wakes up on
the wrong side of the bed one morning, makes a moody remark,
and the entire marketplace believes this to be a harbinger of an
end to easy money: Interest rates skyrocket. The chairman might
have a good day, mentions his belief in bright prospects for the
economy, and the marketplace, accordingly, sighs happily and
interest rates drop.

This is a bit of a caricature, yet one point still stands: Predicting
interest rates and future stock and bond prices is a difficult task.
You've got to bet on so many unpredictables, and then, even if
you're right, the rest of the market may not agree. So your stock
goes down and you're back to where you started. Not to worry,
though, there is one large group who will tell you just when you
should buy.

"Now Is the Time to Buy," Says Mr. Generic Stockbroker

Stockbrokers always say that now is the right time to buy. Here are some quotes to prove my point:

"We will remain in a primarily bull market that will be up again in 1981,"* predicted one analyst in the year-end forecast issue of *Barron's*.

Mario Gabelli, owner of a brokerage house that bears his name, said in a 1981 year-end market report on the coming year, ". . . we're going to have a terrific, exciting market in 1982. I think it will be a great place to make money."†

"Now I happen to think that 1983 and 1984 are going to be wonderful years in the stock market. . . . It's going to get better and better and better,"‡ enthused *Barron's* magazine in the 1982 year-end issue.

"Stocks will go up sharply in the early months of this year [1984] and you should own lots of them,"§ wrote a Thomson Mc-Kinnon Securities vice-president in the December 1983 *Financial World*.

"The stock market . . . should begin the year [1985] in an up-beat mood. . . . Let the good times roll,"‖ various pundits optimistically forecast in the year-end 1984 *Fortune* magazine.

"This will be an up-and-down year. [But] stock prices should hit an all-time high by mid-year,"¶ reported *Money* magazine at the beginning of 1986.

Stockbrokers and market seers are eternal optimists. They have to be able to convince you to put your hard-earned dollars into

---

* "No Double Dip," *Barron's* (January 5, 1981), p. 4.
† "Facing the Future," *Barron's* (December 27, 1982), p. 6.
‡ "Facing the Future," *Barron's* (December 27, 1982), p. 6.
§ Lucian O. Hooper, "Controversial Projects," *Financial World* (New York: Financial World Partners, December 31, 1983), p. 6.
‖ John J. Curran, "Investment Bets for 1985," *Fortune* (New York: Time Inc., December 10, 1984), pp. 191–94.
¶ Jerry Edgerton, "Getting a Fix on 1986," *Money* (New York: Time Inc., January 1986), p. 49.

their investment products. It's wise to remember the stockbroker's adage "Stocks are not bought, they're sold!"

Some years they will be right while in other years they will be wrong. If you always predict sunshine, some days you'll be right and some days you'll be wrong. The same holds true for stockbrokers. They always predict it's going to go up . . . some months they'll be right and sometimes they'll be wrong. Remember this common wisdom whenever you talk with a broker who is interested in selling you his wares.

If you want to buy individual stocks and you want suggestions, a broker is your answer. To find one, simply look through the Sunday business section of your local paper. You should find the phone numbers of the local offices of national brokerage houses. I suggest that you first consider the large national firms. Call up the house on Monday and ask to speak to a broker. Talk to the broker. Tell him or her you'd like to buy some stocks and bonds, state the amount of money you'd like to invest, and ask for current suggestions.

These suggestions, more than likely, will have been recommended to the broker by the firm's research department. That means you're getting the advice along with countless scores of investors across the nation. In other words, what might have been a bargain at one time probably isn't anymore. Don't, whatever you do, invest on the first phone call. Don't invest regardless of how persuasive the broker is or how urgent it is that you invest today, right now, before the opportunity is missed. Ask the broker to send some printed information on his recommendations to you.

When the information arrives look it over. See if what the broker said coincides with the printed information on the stock. Check the price in the newspaper. See how much it has gone up or down since the research report was completed. Be sure to check how old the research report is. If, after all this checking, you like the stock, call up the broker and put in an order. If you can afford it, always buy shares in multiples of 100, a so-called round lot. Whenever you buy an "odd lot," which is to say a group of shares that is not a multiple of 100, you'll pay more money per share.

There are many different kinds of brokers—good ones *and* bad ones, smart ones *and* dumb ones, rich ones *and* not-so-rich ones. It boils down to whether you take to the broker's style. Remember, you can always get another one.

As an alternative to simply calling numbers taken out of the newspaper, ask your friends if they have a broker whom they'd recommend. Call your friends' brokers and go through the same routine. Regardless of what broker you choose and what they say, there are some tricks to stock selection.

My Thoughts

There are three ways to play the market: (1) Pick your own stocks and then go through a discount broker for execution, (2) buy mutual fund shares, (3) find a broker and let him advise and sell you stocks.

I've learned one rule that I abide by religiously: There are no rules that are guarantees. Everyone has a different rule, which, they undoubtedly believe, leads to heretofore unimagined riches: Buy low P/E's, look to the glamour stock, the real high flyers don't set limits; go against the tape, go with the tape; buy little-known stocks, buy only Big Board beauties; buy options and futures, stay as far away from them as you can. There's only one rule that, for the rest of time, will be correct: "Buy low and sell high." However, it's tautological and doesn't tell you how to act or what to do.

There are really only two investing strategies. Under the umbrella of these two broad strategies, there are countless tactics. The first strategy is known as fundamental analysis. The second is called technical analysis. If you used the fundamental analysis technique, you'd assess a company's strengths before buying stock. You could then hold the stock, waiting for the market to pick up on the facts that you have already detected. Because you must wait for the market to recognize the value of the stock, the time horizon for holding a stock is long. The fundamental technique is also called the value approach.

The primary aim of fundamental investors is to find good, quality companies. A quality company is one whose earnings continue to grow at a steady pace. IBM is a good example. For a long time

IBM has held a tight stranglehold on the business computer market. Because of its strength in the computer marketplace and because of the farsightedness of its corporate managers, it has continued to earn more and more money.

This strategy requires sleuthing out companies that continue to show growth in profits. What's important is not the level of profits, but that profits continue to grow. All the market cares about is the future. For that reason, earnings must grow.

By comparison, a technical strategist looks at the relationship between one stock price and the prices of the rest of the securities in the market to determine buy-and-sell signals. The technician does not care about earnings or about future growth potential. He or she simply looks at the trend of trading to determine the future direction. Because prices change constantly, the time horizon of a technical strategy is extremely short.

Technical analysts—and their extreme brethren, the chartists—decipher trends in the movement of stock volumes and prices. C. Colburn Hardy, who writes the yearly compendium of investment information, *Dun & Bradstreet's Guide to Your Investments,* says of technical analysis: "The technical analyst operates on the basis that 1) the action of the stock market is the best indicator of its future course; b) 80% of a stock's price movement is due to factors outside the company's control and 20% to factors unique to that stock; c) the stock market, over a few weeks/months, is rooted 85% in psychology and only 15% in economics."*

Based on their meditations, technicians use an alchemist-like incantation to determine the future direction of stocks. To my mind, technical analysis, unsupported by no more logic than it "goes up because it goes up," is just plain unreliable. Stick to the value approach for picking your stocks. If the industry is good and the company is good, you should make money—regardless of what the dotted lines on a chart look like.

Even if you've got the right company, you've got to worry about the economy and interest rates. And even if you've got the com-

* C. Colburn Hardy, *Dun & Bradstreet's Guide to Your Investments, 1985* (New York: Harper & Row, 1985, 30th edition), p. 133.

pany, the economy, and rates right, you've got to worry about market timing. That's a lot to worry about, indeed. Timing might even be your worst enemy. In a recent *Harvard Business Review* article called "The Folly of Stock Market Timing," the author shows "it only takes a few wrong decisions [about market turns] to deflate the long-term results produced by market timers to the point where the timers would have been just as well off out of the stock market entirely."* Let's have a look at mutual funds.

* Robert H. Jeffrey, "The Folly of Stock Market Timing," *Harvard Business Review* (Boston: President and Fellows of Harvard College, July–August 1984), p. 102.

APPENDIX:
The Risky Business of Options

Stock index options, as respected financial author C. Colburn Hardy puts it, "are the PAC-men" of the securities industry. They are pure, unadulterated bets. Over the last few years option contracts have appeared on various stock indexes. The most popular by far is the Chicago Board of Options Exchange's S&P 100 Index Option. "Of the 122.3 million option contracts traded at the Chicago exchange in 1984, more than 64 million were index options," reports *The Wall Street Journal*. These 64 million trades bet on the future direction of the market. No securities ever trade hands with these options. It's all settled in cash.

With index options you don't worry about individual stock dynamics, you just have to guess which way the market's going to move . . . up or down. With every winner in the index options game, there's a loser. Here's the story of a winner:

Carl Payne graduated in 1984 from a top Ivy League institution. At twenty-three he began working for a building contractor in Washington State. He had been interested in the new financial markets and discovered he could play the game for a sum of money that was not too considerable: $300.

Carl detailed his adventure in stock index options: "Every month or so during 1985, I told a friend that we should 'buy some stock index options. I think that the market's going to go down.'

My friend said, 'Okay, but I think it's going to go up.' We never could agree on the direction, so we didn't play. But, funny thing, I found that his prediction was always right and mine wrong as the Dow Jones Industrial Average kept reaching new highs in 1985.

"Finally, toward the close of 1985, I said, 'I want to play these index options. You've been right all year long, I'll do whatever you say.' He said, 'Up.' I said, 'You're crazy, the market's at a new high, there's got to be some correction.' He said, 'Up.' Like a lemming, I went along.

"With the S&P 100 index standing at 190 at the close of November, the December call options with a strike price of 200 were selling for 5/16ths, or 31.25 cents. We bought option contracts for $281.25 plus a $40 commission. Because the market stood at 190 and we bought options that allowed us to profit if the market went up to 200, we were betting the market was going to go up. For our total investment of $321.25, we bought options on a stock-market portfolio that then had a value of $171,000. This is leverage gone wild. If the market went against us, we stood to lose $321.25—our total investment.

"Over the next week the stock market went up, it went down. At one point the index dropped below 190, so we were out $321.25. The next day the index ascended and we were up $600. On the following day it sagged. Our profit dropped to $80.

"Two weeks later I jumped on the bus to go to work, opened up the newspaper, and flipped to the stock section. The Dow had gone through the roof to a record high. Our index options—we had 900 of these babies [options, not contracts] that we bought for 31 cents—were now selling for $2.125. We were millionaires, or so I felt.

"We earned $1,857.50 [$1,912.50 − $55 commission], or 578 percent on a two-week speculation. Not bad. Several days later, those 31 cent options grew to $7.00. But that's the old story of what could have been.

"Heady with our earlier results, my friend and I teamed up again, only to lose our entire $336 investment on another stock-index foray. There's no story to tell with this one. We bought some contracts at 18.75 cents and watched the market sag. Our options expired, worthless."

Carl was lucky with options. Overall, his gain and his loss netted him and his partner $1,522. His experience is atypical. He made a big hit, his appetite was whetted, and then he lost. It's estimated by sheer numbers. There are ten times more losers than winners in the options game.

When you buy options you're really purchasing an options contract that gives you the *right* to buy or sell 100 shares of the underlying security at a specified price. You do not have the obligation to buy the underlying commodity or security. With options you have the ability or the right to close out the contract, but you don't have to. Clearly, you will close out your contract when you've made a profit and you'll sit on your hands if you're showing a loss.

You can buy options on specific stocks, on bonds, on foreign currency futures, on the consumer price index, and even on stock indexes, such as the S&P 500. Let's look at options on stocks, the easiest to understand. The options on other financial instruments work in essentially the same way.

On January 22, 1986, IBM closed on the New York Stock Exchange at $144.25. At the same time, February call options with a strike price of $150 closed at 1 13/16ths ($1.81). If you owned those particular call options, you would have the right, but not the obligation, to buy IBM stock for $150 per share sometime between January 22 and the third Friday in February. All options that come due in a particular month expire on the third Friday of the specified month.

You would buy that option, that right to buy IBM, if you thought that IBM was going to go over $150 before that third Friday of the following month. If, by chance, IBM stock did go over $150, your right to buy the stock for $150 would suddenly become more valuable. Let's say that IBM stock went to $155 before your option expired. The option that you bought for $1.81 would now be worth at least $5.00 and probably a little more.

First, you could buy the stock outright and pay $155. Or you could exercise your option—that is, turn it in and say "Here's my

$150, give me a share." The first method would cost you $155 plus commissions, whereas the second would cost you only $150 plus the $1.81 it cost you to buy the option, plus some commissions. Excluding commissions, your gain on the second method would be $3.19 (see Chart 26):

CHART 26

Cost to Buy IBM After It Had Risen to $155

	Method 1	Method 2	Method 1 vs. Method 2
Cost of Share	$155.00	$150.00	−$5.00
Cost of Options	0	$1.81	+$1.81
Total Cost	$155.00	$151.81	−$3.19

(Does not include commissions)

Let's go back to January 22, 1986. You want to make the most money you can with your $5,000. You've warmed up your crystal ball and know that IBM is going to go to $155.

If you bought the stock outright, it would cost you $144.25 per share. Excluding commissions, you could have bought about 35 shares. Conversely, you could have bought, at $1.81 per option, approximately 28 options contracts. (Each contract contains options to buy 100 shares.) Your initial investment in each is about the same.

And then, lo and behold, IBM advances to $155. On the shares you've earned $10.75 per share, or 7.5 percent. Not bad for one month's work. On the options, however, you earned $319, or 176 percent, per contract. Here's the scorecard (see Chart 27):

CHART 27

Gain on IBM After It Had Risen to $155

	Method 1 Buy Stocks	Method 2 Buy Options	Method 1 vs. Method 2
Selling Price	$155	$5	$150
Sale	$5,373	$13,812	−$8,439
Cost	$5,000	$5,000	−0−
Gain	$373	$8,812	−$8,439
% Gain Over Cost	7.5%	176%	

Let's look briefly at the downside and say your crystal ball was on the fritz when you made this investment. Instead of shooting up to $155, IBM actually stood firm. The days wore on and the weeks went by. Finally, expiration day for the options arrives. The value of the option on expiration day is worthless. That is, a right to buy IBM for $150 today has absolutely no value when IBM is at $144.25. Here's the scorecard for this possibility (see Chart 28):

CHART 28

Position on IBM After It Had Stayed at $144.25

	Method 1 Buy Stocks	Method 2 Buy Options	Method 1 vs. Method 2
Selling Price	$144.25	$0	$144.25
Sale	$5,000.00	$0	$5,000.00
Cost	$5,000.00	$5,000	$0
Gain	$0	−$5,000	$5,000.00
% Gain	0.0%	−100%	

The risk with the options is much, much greater. In the first example we made 176 percent on our investment in options, while in the second case we lost it all. By contrast, the gain on buying the stock outright in the first case was only 7.5 percent, while in the second case we didn't lose a cent (except for commissions and carrying costs).

You can find options tables in the business section of your newspaper where it lists the options by company. If you look farther down the options table in the newspaper, you'll find that IBM February 155 call options were selling for 13/16ths, or 81.25 cents, while the IBM 160 February call options were priced at 5/16ths, or 31.25 cents. As the strike price goes higher and higher above the current selling price, the chance that the strike price will be reached becomes a lot less likely and, hence, the value of that option, of that right to buy a stock at higher and higher prices, becomes less valuable.

Besides buying the right to buy the stock at a specified price, you can also buy the right to *sell* the stock at a specific price. These are called *put* options. With calls you get to buy the stock while with puts you can sell it.

At the same time as the call options were available, there were also put options on IBM with the same strike price and the same expiration dates. When IBM was selling for $144.25 on the exchange, you could buy February put options with a strike price of $150 for 7³/₈th, or $7.38. This option gives you the right to sell IBM for $150 even though it sold for only $144.25 on the exchange. The intrinsic value of this option was $5.75 ($150 − $144.25). However, because the option still had a month to go before it expired, there was some chance that IBM could go down even farther. The market expressed this possibility: The option cost $7.38 even though the intrinsic value of the right was only $5.75. In other words, the premium for the additional month before expiration was $1.63.

As we step down the option chart (see Chart 29) to the put options exercisable at $155, we find they are even more costly: 11³/₈, or $11.38. Again, the intrinsic value of this right to sell IBM for $155 while the market price of the stock is $144.25 is $10.75 ($155 − 144.25), while the time value equals $.625. The 160 puts sold for $16.

CHART 29

Option Table: Wed., Jan. 22, 1986

Option and N.Y. Close	Strike	Calls		Puts	
		Feb.	Mar.	Feb.	Mar.
144¹/₄	150	1¹³/₁₆	3¹/₂	7³/₈	8⁵/₈
144¹/₄	155	¹³/₁₆	1³/₄	11³/₈	8¹/₄
144¹/₄	160	⁵/₁₆	1	16	12

Among the determinants of an options price is the market value of the stock compared to the strike price of the particular option. If the strike price for a call option—lets you buy the stock—is below the current selling price of the stock, that option is said to be "in the month" or "deep in the month." Similarly, if the strike price for a put—lets you sell the stock—is considerably higher than the current selling price of the stock, that option is also said to be in the money. Conversely, if the option is outside the striking range, the option is said to be "out of the money."

The second determinant of an option's price is the time left before it expires. All other things being equal, the greater the length of time remaining on the option, the more valuable it is. This just makes sense. The more time remaining for the stock to move into the money, the more valuable that right is. On the other hand, even if the stock price remains stagnant, the value of the option is wasting away with the passing of time.

The third criterion for valuing a stock option is how volatile it is. If a stock remains dormant, it's likely that your option will remain out of the money. However, if the stock is given to violent fluctuations, it's more likely that your option will move into the money. Hence, the more volatile the stock, the more costly will be its option.

The point of this excursion into options is to give you a taste of what they are. They're fast-moving, and they're bets. Whenever you take one of these bets, just remember that you're whittling away the money you have available for allowing your nest egg to grow larger and larger. Sure, you may hit, but nine times out of ten, you'll miss. Let's get back to serious investing.

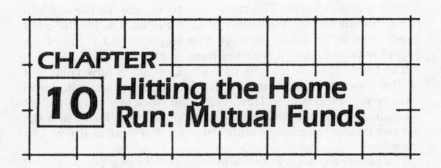

CHAPTER 10
Hitting the Home Run: Mutual Funds

I read a headline buried in *The Wall Street Journal* at the end of 1985. It amazed me not so much because of what it said but for what it implied: "Professional Stock Pickers Are Beating S&P 500 for First Time in Three Years."* The Standard & Poor 500 is the standard gauge of market performance.

Translation: For the last three years people who earn their living choosing stocks were no better at it than a herd of blind chimpanzees with darts.

Another study, this one cited in *Fortune* magazine, points out that "over the previous 15 years, the average yearly performance of two-thirds of these [equity portfolios of major corporate pension funds] funds also trailed the market."†

Again, let me translate. Two thirds of the thousands of college-educated MBA's and Ph.D.'s who pick stocks for a living did worse than you would have had you invested in the securities that make up the S&P 500. For fifteen years you would have done better.

* George Anders, "Professional Stock Pickers Are Beating S&P 500 for First Time in Three Years," *The Wall Street Journal*, December 19, 1985, p. 22.
† "A Mutual Fund that Settles for a Tie," *Fortune*, March 3, 1986, pp. 100–104.

In this chapter we'll solve the problem of choosing an individual stock or bond in which to invest. We'll look at tips and dismiss them out of hand. Your answer is mutual funds. We'll look at what mutual funds are, how to choose among them, and finally we'll conclude with a commonsense investing strategy. The strategy will eliminate much of your downside risk and, with the correct choice of a mutual fund, should enhance your upside potential.

Before discussing the investment strategies implied by the sage business sources cited above, let's quickly review what the S&P 500 is. The S&P index is computed in the same way mutual funds are. Its full name is the Standard & Poor's 500-Stock Index. The index is a collection of 400 industrial, 40 utility, 20 transportation, and 40 financial services stocks.

Most of these stocks trade on the New York Stock Exchange. Each is weighted in the index according to its market capitalization. In plainspeak that means the number of shares outstanding for each stock is multiplied by its most recent selling price. This constitutes the market value of the stocks. These values are added together each nanosecond to determine a new index value. The following chart shows the largest ten stocks in the S&P 500 and adds in the value of the other 490 stocks (see Chart 30):

CHART 30

Largest 10 Stocks in the S&P 500

Name of Company	Number of Shares ×	Market Price =	Market Capital	% of S&P Index
IBM	615	$146.50	$90,185	5.1%
Exxon	724	$60.88	$44,069	2.5%
AT&T	1,069	$25.38	$27,134	1.5%
General Motors	318	$77.63	$24,667	1.4%

Largest 10 Stocks in the S&P 500

Name of Company	Number of Shares ×	Market Price =	Market Capital	% of S&P Index
Royal Dutch Petroleum	268	$80.50	$21,576	1.2%
E. I. DuPont	241	$83.50	$20,148	1.1%
Bell South	314	$62.75	$19,741	1.1%
Phillip Morris	239	$74.63	$17,859	1.0%
Sears, Roebuck	366	$48.50	$17,731	1.0%
Total Value of 10 Stocks			$283,110	18.0%
Total Market Value of the 500 Stocks			$1,778,080	100%
/Divisor (Base value)			$7,088	
—Index Value			$250.8	

On the day that the above index was calculated, the value of all shares of companies in the index was multiplied by the number of shares outstanding. The divisor turns the gross market value into an index: 250.8. This isn't arcane stuff. It is largely the same way the value of a mutual fund's shares are calculated.

On any given day you can determine how well or how poorly the market is doing as compared to the day before. For instance, let's say that the price of the shares on the top-ten list increased from one day to the next *and* the index rose 25.9 points, or slightly more than 10 percent, to 275.9. Thus, we would say that the market rose 10 percent from one day to the next. This is the gauge against which all investors should measure themselves. This is the stock market.

Hot-Shot MBA vs. Joe-Average Investor

For many years it has been consistently shown that by investing in all 500 stocks that comprise the index, you will earn a market rate of return while diversifying away much of the risk inherent in owning one or two securities. Thus, despite all the work of security analysts, despite all the dog-and-pony shows by corporate presidents, and despite all the work of the countless multitudes in the security business, your Joe-average investor can easily perform as well as the market, and many times better than the professionals.

To invest in all 500 stocks isn't tough. It doesn't require an MBA, Ph.D., CPA, or any other combination of letters. All it takes is a phone call to a mutual fund house or a broker that offers an index fund. You say "I want to buy the S&P 500." For three straight years you would have done better on the average than professional portfolio managers. Period. No guessing about interest rates. No guessing about the stream of earnings twenty years in the future. No guessing about which side of the bed the head of the Federal Reserve woke up on. Nothing.

The *Journal* article cited at the beginning of this chapter asserted that "money managers guide more than $1 trillion in pension assets, collecting several *billion dollars* [emphasis added] of annual fees."* Robert Wade, chief investment officer for Citicorp —the nation's largest banking institution—added sheepishly, "The S&P has been a very tough target the past few years." The *Journal* added that Citicorp expended millions upon millions of dollars annually trying to outsmart the market.

You might ask yourself, If the largest bank in the nation can't do it, even when spending more money than the gross national product of several smaller countries, how can you, Joe-average, small investor, do it?

I think this is very telling and highly suggestive of how you

---

* George Anders, "Professional Stock Pickers are Beating S&P 500 for First Time in Three Years," *The Wall Street Journal,* December 19, 1985, p. 22.

ought to run your own portfolio. You may be able to beat the market. That also means, however, that someone else on the other side isn't beating the market. How can you be so sure you'll be the one on top? You can't. Of course, I'm not suggesting that you dig a hole in your backyard and bury your money.

Over the last fifty years common stocks or equities have on the average returned six percentage points more than risk-free Treasury bills each year. There have been dramatic swings indeed. Some years the return from stocks was actually less than that of T-bills. Other years have more than compensated for this. Over the long haul, since the 1920s, the S&P 500 has returned six percentage points more than risk-free T-bills.* There's money to be made in equities. But how?

Tips?

You can make a bundle with options. Or you can lose your stake (see appendix to Chapter 9). You can watch your investment go through the roof with foreign currency futures, or you can spend restless nights waiting for margin calls. A friend calls you with a tip: "Psst, buy Merrill Lynch, there's takeover talk in the air. GM. Citicorp. I don't know. Whatever you do, buy now." Or: "I got this friend, he's working on the deal, you gotta buy now."

Funny thing about tips. Undoubtedly, by the time you, on the outer fringes of the investment community, hear the tip, everyone inside the industry will have already heard the tip. If you act impulsively and buy on the tip, you're probably buying the stock from someone who heard the tip a week earlier.

If you happen to hear the tip from the president of a company who told you his firm is either about to be taken over or will soon announce it's filing for bankruptcy, and you act on the tip, you might find an agent from the Securities and Exchange Commission (SEC) at your door. Acting on a real inside tip is illegal. Just ask Dennis Levine.

* Burton G. Malkiel, *A Random Walk Down Wall Street* (New York: Norton & Company, 1981: 2nd college edition), p. 191.

As I write this Mr. Levine has just been sentenced to two years in prison for insider trading. An accomplice, Ivan Boesky, was forced to pay fines totalling $100 million on the same charges. Insider trading occurs when you act on information that has not yet been released to the public. Mr. Levine allegedly garnered $12 million in ill-gotten profits through the creation of a dummy bank account in the Bahamas, which then filtered money through a Swiss bank account. Quite an intricate scheme—yet, he got caught.

Usually when a company is about to be taken over the selling price rises dramatically before the announcement. This implies that the tip network is active. Someone involved in the takeover, or someone who is peripherally related to the takeover (secretaries, janitors, clerks), learned of the takeover before the announcement. When they learned that the firm was being taken over, they or their friends and family went into the marketplace and bought the security. This is illegal. A presidential aide recently went to prison for conducting his personal financial affairs in a similar manner. Even if you think you are far enough away from the actual takeover transaction, you probably won't get away with it. Just ask Dennis Levine or Ivan Boesky or any of a myriad of people who were arrested on insider trading charges in 1986 and 1987.

Then there is always the question about whether the takeover is really going to happen. You can bet many smart people have lost more than a pittance on all the deals that were touted as sure-fire happenings but were never consummated. If the takeover does happen, will the price be high enough to justify your buying the stock at an already inflated price? Finally, how can you be sure you're not at the tail end of the tip and that everyone before you has run up the price to the point where, tip or no tip, you'll lose money?

And then there's the tip that is nothing more than an act of manipulation. At one time I was intimately involved in the penny stock market that operated principally out of Denver. Penny stocks are shares that trade in the Over-the-Counter market, usually for less than a dollar. That's why they're called penny stocks.

Typically these companies are start-up companies that haven't earned a single dollar in revenues.

The two mainstays of the penny market used to be high-tech and energy firms. These high-tech firms promised to produce revolutionary items like a thermometer that takes your temperature just by looking at you or a computerized cash register that every restaurant in the world would simply have to buy. Promoters of these ventures spoke with confidence about the untold billions that would flow into company coffers once the world learned about these great new advances.

There were also irresistible oil and gas firms. I laughed at these as well. Drilling for oil or gas is extremely risky in unproven fields. While there are all sorts of scientific methods for determining how likely it will be that there is oil or gas in the ground, it's still largely a matter of punching a hole in the ground and crossing your fingers.

If a well struck oil, the rumors about the size of the pool would fly across the penny-stock houses in Denver and across the country. I've heard of enough gushers containing such vast pools that the entire continent of North America would be flooded with oil. These were tall tales.

Broker: Psst. I know that the hit is so big, it could equal all of Saudi Arabia's and then some.
Me: Ah, come on.
Broker: No, this one is really big. It's the new Anadarko Basin. And this firm has all the rights.
Me: How much is the stock trading for?
Broker: Twenty-five cents, forty cents.
Me: If it's such a big hit, why's the stock so cheap?
Broker: Because no one knows about it yet.
Me: You know about it, and now I know about it.

The stories went on and on. Most brokers were honest and had just got suckered into the story. With every retelling the level of the virtually assured revenues just grew and grew.

What do you do with such a tip? You might bet a little. You

might bet a lot. However, even if you bet a little, say $300 to $500, you could cause a setback in your more serious portfolio. If you're starting with $3,000 in your portfolio, a loss of $300 equals a negative 10 percent after-tax return. (The math isn't altogether correct because you gain the tax benefit of a capital loss. In reality, say you're in a combined federal, state, and local tax bracket of 35 percent; your $300 loss is offset by a $105 reduction in your tax bill. Hence, you suffer a −7 percent after-tax loss.)

Financial planner C. Colburn Hardy astutely points out that "for every 50% loss, [you] have to make 100% profit on the next deal just to break even."* Why chance it? You could take a vacation, a sure thing, with that money. If you're setting out to buy a house, every little bit counts.

Tips are bad news. The preceding information on investing in stocks was a long-winded way to sell you on safe, proven mutual funds. They eliminate virtually all the investment problems I've detailed in this and the previous chapter.

A Proven Suggestion, Not a "Tip"

Mutual funds provide diversity, security, and convenience. If you don't have countless hours and a career to spend deciphering the cryptic ways of the stock market, I truly believe that mutual funds are for you. Even if you are an amateur stock-market enthusiast, you're more likely to come out ahead with mutual funds than by picking your own stocks. Let's look at the nuts and bolts of mutual fund investing.

A mutual fund is a company. This company sells shares to the public to raise money. Like any other publicly held company, it is owned by its shareholders.

Depending on its particular objectives, this company may buy and sell stocks, bonds, commercial paper, options, or other securities. It earns its money through buying low and selling high. Any gains made on securities are passed through to the mutual fund's

---

* C. Colburn Hardy, *The Facts of Life: The Young Professional's Guide to Financial Planning* (New York: Amacom, 1986), p. v.

owners. Any losses it incurs are also passed through to the investors.

You, as a shareholder, hire a management company to run the mutual fund company for you. These managers earn a service fee from you, the owner. These service fees constitute the management expenses for running the company for its owners. The mutual fund company raises money to make these investments from investors. The mutual fund company raises money from investors, its shareholders, to make investments on their behalf. Because the fund pools money from many, many investors, it is able to diversify to a much greater extent than you could on your own.

The minimum investment for mutual funds ranges from $1,000 to $3,000. After you have opened your account, you can withdraw money, thereby allowing your balance to dip below this amount. In other words, if you don't have the minimum handy, you could borrow money to open the account and then sell back most of it to cover the loan. Nobody in the mutual fund industry will tell you that and, if they ask, I didn't tell you either.

You can choose from among 1,200 funds. The amount invested in mutual funds has exploded over the last few years. Net sales (additions to the funds less reductions) grew from slightly less than $2 billion in 1980 to over $30 billion in 1985. That's up 1,400 percent.*

This rapid growth is due in part to investors placing their Individual Retirement Account (IRA) capital in the funds and small institutions using mutual funds to manage their capital. The real reason for the explosion is that investors are becoming wise to the notion that it's very, very hard to beat the market. It is extremely difficult to find those one or two or twenty stocks that will do better than the market. Picking individual stocks remains a dicey proposition over the short run.

You can choose from a multitude of funds. Some might say that your choice of funds depends on your risk tolerance. I would ar-

* Laura R. Walbert, "The Roaring '80's," *Forbes* (New York: September 16, 1985), pp. 76–79.

gue that it really isn't as important as it first might sound after you weed out some crazy funds.

Mutual funds are incredibly convenient these days. They operate like a savings or a money market account. Non-bank money market accounts are in fact a special kind of mutual fund. Typically, you can get a book that looks remarkably like a checkbook from which you can write drafts—which are very similar to checks—to pay for purchases over some minimum amount, usually $250 or $500.

Loading Up—Act 1

There are two basic varieties of mutual funds to buy: load funds and no-load funds. "Load" is a term that someone, somewhere dreamed up to avoid calling it a sales charge. Most funds have a front-end load, which means that any time you buy shares in the fund, you'll have to pay a commission. Typically, this amounts to 8.5 percent of your investment. In recent days a new mischievous arrangement has come on the scene. It's called a back-end load. You call your broker to sell your mutual fund shares and he charges you a commission to sell. Some funds charge a fee for reinvesting your earnings into the fund. Norman Fosback, editor of the mutual fund newsletter, *The Mutual Fund Forecaster*, calls these "reloading charges."

In a no-load fund, however, you don't pay sales charges or commissions when you move in or out of the fund. I know of no reason to buy shares in a fund that charges a load or sales charge —front or back or reload.

The larger houses have toll-free 800 numbers. To make an investment in a no-load mutual fund, call them up and request a prospectus. A prospectus is just a description of the fund. It tells you who manages it and includes information on the past performance, and it usually comes with an application. If you know which prospectus you're interested in, you can request the specific prospectus. I'd recommend having them send you prospectuses for all their funds.

Read the prospectuses when they arrive. You'll join a select

few. The director of SEC Investment Management Division,
Kathryn McGrath, estimates that less than 10 percent of mutual
fund investors even read the title page of the prospectus.* It is the
legal document by which securities firms can sell their investment
wares. When you see a notice in a newspaper informing you
about a mutual fund, don't be misled into thinking that this is an
advertisement. It's really not an ad. It's just an offer to send you
the ad.

In this offering circular you'll get a description of the overriding
objectives of the fund: income, growth, aggressive growth, tax-
free growth, tax-free income, growth and income, and so on.
(We'll look at what this means in greater detail shortly.)

Second, you'll get a description of the fund's policies outlining
how it plans to meet the objectives cited above. You'll also find an
account of how the fund's moneys are handled and by whom. I
pay special attention to this section. It describes the ladies and
gentlemen who'll be running your money (hopefully, not running
with your money). You should investigate whether any of the people involved in the fund have ever been asked by the SEC or the
National Association of Securities Dealers (NASD) to step out of
the securities business for any period of time.

Make sure no lawsuits are pending against the fund, and you
should be wary if lawsuits have been filed in the past—even if the
fund has won those suits. Legal troubles are not a good sign. By
and large, those in the securities industry are honest and hard-
working. But there are always some bad apples. Even if the suit
has been settled in the fund's favor, you can find many, many
funds that have not been tainted at all. As far as your money is
concerned, you have enough to worry about with seeking the best
return. You don't need the added problems of a company with
legal problems—past or present. If you see even the slightest indication of legal problems, look to another prospectus and another
fund. There are many.

If the fund's been around for a while, you should look at its

* "Money Talks," *Money* (New York: Time Inc., vol. 15, no. 9, September 1986), p.
13.

performance history. At the end of each quarter popular financial magazines such as *Forbes, Money,* and *Business Week* run performance comparisons on the various mutual funds. Use these to comparison shop. Don't allow the results from just one quarter to sway your decision. *Forbes* magazine advises, "Buying the fund that was up the most last year is a prescription for trouble. Many a fund that buys high risk, fast moving stocks looks brilliant in a bull market but loses its investors huge sums in the inevitable bear market that follows."*

The next section of the prospectus describes how to buy into the fund. This is usually a simple matter, accomplished by filling out a form. The form will ask your name, your mailing address, and several other innocuous pieces of information, and then will inquire whether you want a checkbook and the option of being able to wire money directly to and from your bank account. The fund wants to make it convenient for you. One choice you face is the disposition of your investment returns. Almost regardless of fund type, your fund will pay dividends and capital gains. The fund can send you a check each time or it can reinvest the money in the fund for you. Choose to reinvest. You don't need the current income and it's better not to have that money in your checking account where you can spend it. The one catch, however, is that at the end of the year, you have to pay taxes on those dividends even though you reinvested them.

And, oh yes, there's the check. On the form it will tell you the minimum amount necessary to open the account and the amount necessary for subsequent investments. I've found that I can send the fund any amount of money for subsequent investments and they will take it. (Again, you didn't hear that from me.) You do have to send them that first minimum check. This may make you feel uncomfortable. Mutual funds, unlike bank accounts, are not insured by any agency. If they go broke, you may not see your money again.

Once you've sent in your money, you'll receive a confirmation

---

* "The Honor Roll—1986 Annual Mutual Funds Survey," *Forbes* (New York: Forbes, Inc., vol. 138, no. 5, September 8, 1986), p. 110.

notice and you're on your way to earning solid returns year after year. Any time there is activity in your account you'll receive a statement from the fund sponsor. Your statement will note how you started off the month, the additional investments you made, any money you took out of the fund, any distributions (i.e., dividends or capital gains) credited to your account, and how you finished off the month. Your statement will also detail the number of shares you own.

Distributions and Net Asset Value

You invest in a mutual fund for two reasons: to earn distributions and positive changes in net asset value. Huh? As a shareholder in this mutual fund company, you're entitled to any dividends that the company receives. Let's say the mutual fund company bought General Motors stock and GM pays its annual dividend. You are entitled to a percentage of that dividend. Your portion of the dividend will either be sent directly to you or reinvested in your account. As suggested above, you, the young investor, should have chosen the reinvestment option.

The other critical parameter is the net asset value. This refers to the value of your shares. The net asset value is the total dollar value of the stock portfolio divided by the number of shares outstanding:

$$\frac{\text{Total Market Value of Portfolio}}{\text{Number of Mutual Fund Shares Outstanding}} = \frac{\text{Net}}{\text{Asset}}\ \text{Value}$$

Your fund takes the money you invest, checks the current net asset value (abbreviated NAV in the newspapers), and then credits you with the number of shares that your money can buy. You don't have to worry about buying a round lot of shares (multiples of 100). Hundredths of a share can be purchased. On receiving the information that the fund managers have more money to invest, they seek out additional investments on the open market, thereby balancing the new dollars with the total value of the portfolio.

For example, let's say that Big Blow Mutual Fund's shares have a net asset value today of $10 and there are 100,000 shares out-standing. The aggregate value of the stock portfolio chosen by the fund's managers is $1 million, and they have no uninvested funds —i.e., no cash—lying around:

Net Asset Value
  of Shares   Number of Shares   Portfolio Value + Cash
  $10   ×   100,000   = $1,000,000 + 0

You show up tomorrow with your check for $1,000 and say, "I want in." The fund managers smile, take your check, and try to figure out what to do. First, they put it in their cash account and credit you with 100 shares ($1,000 divided by $10 per share equals 100 shares). Accordingly, they've added $1,000 to the fund's as-sets while outstanding shares increased by 100. Hence, the net asset value remains at $10:

Net Asset Value
  of Shares   Number of Shares   Portfolio Value + Cash
  $10   ×   100,000 + 100   = $1,000,000 + $1,000

Later that day they go into the marketplace, figure out what interest rates are going to do, and predict company earnings.

Let's say they buy $1,000 worth of stock in Apple Computer. The trade goes through. They reduce their cash position and in-crease the portfolio value:

Net Asset Value
  of Shares   Number of Shares   Portfolio Value + Cash
  $10   ×   100,000 + 100   = $1,001,000 + 0

Then the next day begins. Some stocks go up, some go down. Apple goes both up and down. Because of the increase in the value of stocks in the fund's portfolio, the portfolio's value has risen by $19,000 to $1,020,000 by the end of the day. That's an increase of 1.9 percent. Since there are still 100,100 shares out-standing, the net asset value rises to $10.19:

$$\frac{\text{Portfolio Value} + \text{Cash}}{\text{Number of Shares}} = \frac{\$1,020,000 + 0}{100,100} = \text{Net Asset Value} = \$10.19$$

You've made a capital gain of 19 cents, or 1.9 percent. Not bad for a day's work. If you could get that to happen every day for a year—hello, easy street—you'd earn 963 percent. But that doesn't happen, so forget it.

There are two ways that your investment grows in a mutual fund: Either the fund distributes dividends and capital gains *or* the net asset value increases. The fund's value does not improve because of an increase in the number of shareholders or in their investment. (This is true only for open-ended funds. Closed-end funds do not offer new shares. The value of shares is a function of supply and demand for the existing shares.) If that were to occur, it would be a Ponzi scheme, where today's investors are rewarded with tomorrow's shareholder investments. For open-ended mutual funds, the net asset value increases only if the underlying portfolio moves up.

Getting your money back is easy. There are three ways to achieve this. First, you can simply write a draft (looks like a check) from your draft book. When the draft hits your account at the mutual fund house, they determine the current net asset value and redeem the appropriate number of shares. Second, you can call up your fund and have the fund sponsors wire the money to your bank (if you've chosen that option and have arranged it with your bank when you first opened the account). Again, the fund managers redeem the appropriate number of shares. Third, you can write a letter requesting that a redemption check be sent.

The ease of redeeming shares is a prime reason for buying into a mutual fund in the first place: liquidity. Mutual funds are legally obligated to give you access to your account any time they are open for business. For the no-loads, you don't have to play costly games such as markups, markdowns, or commissions, as you will when you buy and sell stocks through a broker.

The other big benefit from mutual funds is diversity. The fund pools your money with millions, if not hundreds of millions, of other investors' dollars, allowing you to play the market in a big way.

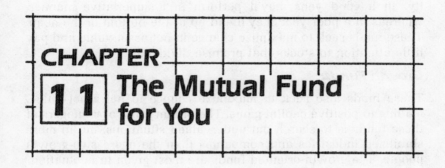

CHAPTER

11 The Mutual Fund for You

In this chapter, we zero in on picking the right mutual fund for you. At the completion of this chapter, you'll know exactly what fund is right for you—along with the number to call to get an application to buy shares in the fund.

There are many, many different brands of funds available to choose from. There are ten generic types of funds. The distinctions among them blur at times. In the statement of principles found in the prospectus, you can find management's objectives. The ten fund types are:

1. Aggressive growth funds
2. Growth funds
3. Growth and income funds
4. Balanced funds
5. Income funds
6. Bond funds
7. Municipal bond funds
8. Specialty funds
9. Money market mutual funds
10. Tax-exempt money market funds

Aggressive Growth Funds:

These funds are the riskiest—that is, they endure the most volatility. In a good year they'll perform in a superlative manner, whereas in a poor year they'll end up at the bottom of the heap. These funds seek to maximize change in net asset value and pay little attention to stocks that promise dividends.

Growth Funds:

These funds also seek to maximize change in net asset value, leading to positive capital gains. The primary aim of managers of these funds is to search out undervalued situations, but in more stabilized industries and companies than the aggressive-growth people. The growth-oriented funds are most given to fluctuation.

Growth and Income Funds:

The best of both worlds. They seek balance by investing in firms that offer capital gains and in those that have a steady history of dividend payouts.

Balanced Funds:

These funds seek balance and harmony. In principle, these funds are less risky than those listed above. They aim for growth in net asset value and a higher income level through dividends by investing in growth stocks, dividend stocks, preferred stocks, and bonds. Preserving investor capital is a critical foundation of these funds.

Income Funds:

These funds are primarily concerned with achieving high income levels for investors. They are, I would argue, primarily for retirees who are (1) no longer concerned about tax brackets and (2) need income from investments for daily living purposes.

Bond Funds:

1985 turned the bond market on its head. Falling interest rates spurred the bond market to new highs. (Remember what I told you, falling interest rates cause bond prices to rise.) Interest-rate volatility over the last several years has caused extreme gyrations in bond prices. As a result, good old safe bonds, which had heretofore been an investment that generated a solid, safe income stream, suddenly became a tool for achieving substantial capital gains. *Forbes* magazine, which conducts an annual survey, showed that from September 1984 to September 1985, the S&P 500 returned 30.9 percent in income and capital gains whereas the Merrill Lynch bond index showed a return of 29 percent for the same period.* In principle, a bond fund buys corporate bonds and seeks income as opposed to capital gains. Junk-bond funds are riskier; fund sponsors invest in less credit-worthy issues.

Municipal Bond Funds:

These funds invest in bonds issued by local government and regional agencies, such as water authorities. Investment in these funds has shown the highest growth in the mutual fund industry of late. Income from these securities is not taxed by the federal government and the tax advantages are passed on to investors in the fund. While fund income is free from federal taxation, it is still subject to the more feeble—yet, grasping—hand of state and local tax collectors. Remember, though, that while the *income* is not subject to federal taxation, *capital gains* are.

Does it make more sense to buy a municipal bond fund whose income is tax free than a corporate bond fund whose income is subject to taxation? It's first a function of your tax bracket. You live in an after-tax world. If you're in a 28 percent federal tax bracket, you pay 28 cents of every incremental dollar to the government. Multiply the taxable corporate bond fund return by 72 percent (100 percent − 28 percent) to determine whether you should get into a tax-free fund or not. For example, *Forbes*'s 1986 study of corporate bonds showed a 9.9 percent return from dividends. On the other hand, the municipal bond index returned 8.2 percent from dividends. If you had had the foresight to forecast

---

* "1985 Fund Ratings," *Forbes*, September 16, 1985, pp. 98–150.

this information at the start of 1985, this would have been your calculation:

CORPORATE BONDS	TAX-FREE BONDS
Taxable Return = 9.9%	Tax-Free Return = 8.2%
Tax Paid on Taxable Return	No Tax Paid on Tax-Free Return
28% × 9.9% = 2.8%	0%
After-Tax Return	After-Tax Return
9.9% − 2.8% = 7.1%	8.2% − 0% = 8.2%

It would have been beneficial for you, the investor in a 28 percent tax bracket, to have put your funds into the tax-free fund.

Specialty Funds:

In the last several years, along with the diversification and expansion of the mutual fund industry, several new, so-called specialty funds have been started. Several invest solely in penny stocks. Others use stock options to assure a certain return on their market portfolio. Some invest solely in companies that mine gold, while other socially responsible funds stay out of industries with questionable practices. These funds are born under certain premises that, more than simply growth or income, dictate their investment practices. Prima facie, these funds are riskier because they are limited by investment criteria from fully diversifying across the wide spectrum of available investments. However, an industry-by-industry examination is really warranted to determine whether the fund is more or less risky than a big basket of stocks.

Money Market Mutual Funds:

These, too, are mutual funds, at least the ones not run by banks. Money market funds invest in very short-term bonds or notes. These notes usually mature in 90 to 180 days. A bond fund, on the other hand, purchases bonds that do not come due until anywhere from five to twenty years. The market values of bonds in bond funds are subject to swings because of potential gyrations in interest rates. However, money market mutual funds purchase commercial paper—a type of loan that typically expires in less than

180 days. As a result, the value of the bond does not change much as the income or interest on the loan is specified in advance and will be paid.

Banks over the last few years began offering money market accounts. With bank money market funds, your money is insured by the appropriate state or federal agency. With non-bank money market funds, it is not insured. Some non-bank money market funds have arranged for insurance companies to insure their money market fund assets. As a general rule, though, because non-bank money market funds are not insured, you can expect to earn a slightly higher interest rate from non-bank money market accounts.

However, generally speaking, bank and non-bank money market funds offer only slightly higher returns than an average savings account. You should keep your savings and investment money in a money market fund only if you need the money within a short time. Otherwise, there are funds that offer considerably higher returns without much trade-off in risk, such as a medium-term bond fund.

Tax-Free Money Market Funds:

These are the newest hybrid to show up on the investment scene. These are money market funds that purchase short-term government paper. Like municipal bond funds, the income they return is free from federal taxation. Some fund houses sell specialized money market funds. These funds purchase short-term paper from select municipalities. At this writing they have shown up in high population areas such as New York City, California, and Illinois. Over time we'll probably see them wherever there's enough investor interest. The benefit is obvious if you happen to live in one of these jurisdictions. As a single person living in New York City, I am subject to the most onerous tax rate that a person can be in in this great country of ours. For that reason I keep some of my short-term money in a fund that keeps me out of the taxation heat of three governments—New York City, New York State, and the federal government—bearing down on me.

The decision about whether to keep your short-term money in a tax-free fund again depends on your tax bracket and on the expected return from the tax-free fund as opposed to a fully taxable one. Of course you shouldn't keep all that much money in a money market fund in the first place. Accordingly, the difference between the return from a taxable money market fund and the tax-free ones, in absolute dollars, should be minimal at best.

Loading Up—Act II

In the last chapter, I made a serious assertion. To refresh your memories, it was "I know of no reason to buy shares in a fund that charges a load or sales charge." Now I'm going to back it up.

When you make your initial venture into the mutual fund market, you should be wary of the "load." Most likely you won't hear a peep about the existence of no-load funds from your broker. Sponsors of mutual funds earn their living through the management fees, which are charged against the income a fund earns before you see it on your statements through distributions. It does not matter one iota how often you invest, withdraw money, or switch accounts. The no-load fund deducts expenses from income generated per share. The load funds do that as well.

A broker will not sell you a no-load fund. Brokers are in business to earn commissions. (At this writing discount broker Charles Schwab, Inc. is offering a service that allows investors to switch among mutual funds at will. For this service the brokerage house adds a load to the no-load funds.) But regardless of whether you make any money, they earn theirs by convincing you to buy and sell. It's no surprise, then, that the broker will try to sell you a loaded fund. Of the funds currently in operation, 64 percent are load funds. That also means that 36 percent of the funds are no-load funds. You therefore have an option. With the no-load fund you'll have to do a little work on your own, namely calling the fund's sponsor yourself and getting brochures and applications sent to you. In either case you'll still have to fill out the form.

Here's why I say go with no-load funds. Load funds do no better than the no-load variety. But those loads can add up. Most loads amount to 8.5 percent at the front end of your investment. (Of course we already understand about the back-end load, which usually amounts to the same thing.) So 8.5 percent of your investment ends up as a brokerage commission.

Every year *Forbes* magazine computes an honor roll of mutual funds that have consistently done very, very well. To make the honor roll in 1985 required an eight-and-three-quarter-year average annual return of at least 20 percent and an excellent performance in both up and down markets. Twenty-three funds made the list. I preformed an analysis of the honor roll and excluded five funds because they were closed to new investors. Of the eighteen remaining funds, eleven had loads ranging from 3 to 8.5 percent. The loaded funds had an annual average return over nearly nine years of 23.9 percent. The other seven funds were no-loads and their average annual return was 23.4 percent. In sum, the returns from the loaded mutual funds favored the ones without a sales charge by slightly more than one half of a percentage point.

Here's the real clincher. *Forbes* then went the next step and asked, If a hypothetical high-tax-bracket investor had invested $10,000 in 1976, how much would his portfolio be valued at today, including sales charges (the load) and taxes? For the loaded group of funds the value of the $10,000 invested in 1976 would have been $52,569. However, for the no-load group the average value of the portfolio would have been $55,277—$2,708 or 5 percent better (see Chart 31):

CHART 31

Forbes's 1985 Mutual Fund Survey Results
(Hypothetical)

	Portfolio in 1976	Portfolio in 1985	Nine-Year Average Return
No-Load	$10,000	$55,277	23.37%
Load	$10,000	$52,569	23.94%

Here's an even better clincher: The loaded-fund results were buoyed by one fund in particular, the Fidelity Magellan Fund, which is managed by Peter Lynch, a superstar in the mutual fund industry. His fund charges a 3 percent load. During the nine-year study period for the *Forbes* survey, his fund averaged a 33 percent annual return, with the hypothetical $10,000 investment equaling $103,139, a 931 percent gain. If we don't include Mr. Lynch's results with the rest of the loaded-fund group, we find that the average annual return drops to 23.04 percent, slightly worse than the no-load group. And, the final step, if we take out his nine-year, $10,000-to-$103,139 return, the value of the loaded portfolio drops to $47,512. In other words, by disregarding this one fund's return, the no-load group of funds outperformed the loaded group by a full $7,765, or 16 percent.

Here's what salespersons pushing loaded funds will say: "First, don't pay any attention to McWilliams. Second, because we charge you for the services, we pay special attention to that fund's results. If we don't do that and the fund underperforms, you'll go elsewhere."

Malarkey. The people who manage the loaded portfolios are just investment managers who are very much like the people who run the no-load portfolios. Their job is to get the best possible return. The salesperson is really trying to convince you that he'll pay attention to your return and, if necessary, switch funds among those his firm manages so you'll get the best return consistent with your own goals.

There are two arguments for using a loaded fund sold through your broker. First, you don't have to send a check through the mail to a faceless institution. Second, a broker can help you make a selection from a short list of funds that he shows you.

For no-load funds, I can't eliminate the necessity of sending the check through the mail. However, to aid in selection I will give you a short list of mutual funds later in the chapter. You'll be able to make your own, informed choice from this select list, which includes only no-load funds.

How Do I Choose One?

There are two broad parameters that dictate which fund you choose. The first is performance while the second is consistency. Every year, every mid-year, and usually every quarter, you can find mutual fund performance summaries. Typically, these will cite the total assets invested in the fund and include a record of the most recent period's performance as well as a longer-term performance measure, such as three years or five years.

When you consider mutual funds you should also concern yourself with the consistency of the fund's results. That is, has the fund consistently outperformed the market in both good and bad years? Often with five-year results it's tough to know whether the fund performed erratically from year to year. Beware of those funds that only tell you how they've done since the mid-1970s and early 1980s. These were bottom years for the stock market, and any fund that hasn't performed well since those benchmark years should be dismissed. You'll have to do a little digging to determine how well the fund has performed in bad years as well as good. A good benchmark is the S&P 500 and its performance. Often the mutual fund's brochure will compare its return for the year with the S&P 500.

I once sat in with a financial adviser who gave me a list of funds from which to choose. He had picked several funds that his company managed. I went through the list and circled those that had the highest return. "Which one should I buy?" I asked.

He shrugged his shoulders and replied, "They're all good."

Phooey to that. They're not all good. Some charge a load. Some have low P/E's and others have high ones. Some have high management fees relative to the total investment managed (called the expense-to-asset ratios) that are astronomical. Some perform exceedingly well in the first year and go downhill from there. Some do great in bull markets and fall precipitously in bad ones. There *are* differences among mutual funds.

Past Is Prologue

Whenever you read anything that even smells of securities, you'll see the proviso "Past Results Are No Indication of Future Results." This little adage is demanded by the SEC. But while everyone includes this, they do so with a wink. If you're not to look at past results as an indication of future results, what are you supposed to look at? Of course past results are an indicator of future results.

I believe that mutual funds are the way to go for young people with some money on their hands who are looking to get ahead. Picking an individual stock is a lot like playing the lottery. When you pick an individual stock the large institutions—the pension funds, the large bank trusts, even mutual funds—may have different plans for your chosen stock than you would like.

But when you invest in mutual funds you've got the big boys on your side. The investment managers think they *can* beat the market. Some of them—albeit a select few—have. Let them worry about what interest rates are going to do. Let them enjoy the lunches that go along with dog-and-pony shows corporate presidents put on. Let them stay up sleepless nights worrying about the direction of stock prices. When you buy into a mutual fund you have only two worries—which one to choose and when to disengage. There are only two times to withdraw your money from the fund: (1) when you need to buy your home or other real estate or (2) when the fund stops performing at the top.

Here comes my disclaimer. The mutual funds market may not be for you. I don't know your personal financial situation. If you have no money to invest or if you know with certainty that you'll need the money for rent, food, or clothes within six months, for goodness' sake, stay out of the mutual fund market.

But if you have the minimum to invest, you can afford to lose up to 20 or 30 percent of it, and if you're looking to watch your investment portfolio grow over time, then a mutual fund is your best bet.

Here's my advice: Buy the S&P 500 index fund or one of

Forbes's Honor Roll no-load members designated below. These funds have consistently earned 20 percent or greater in each year from 1976 to 1985.

The Vanguard Group offers an index fund—a mutual fund comprised only of the stocks that make up the S&P 500. In 1985 the annual expenses charged by the Vanguard Group for management services were 27 cents per $100 in assets. By far and away this is the lowest expense associated with any mutual fund. Most funds average between $1.00 and $1.50 per $100 in expenses. (I have no ties to the Vanguard Group. I don't know anybody that works there, though I do keep some of my investments in several of their funds. If you invest in the index fund, it will not affect my investments with this group in any manner.) And with the index fund you know you'll beat two thirds of the mutual funds on the market.

You're in this game to get ahead and will be taking some risks. If an index fund isn't for you, here's another list. I didn't come up with it—*Forbes* magazine did. I selected it because it's the best.

The Honor Roll

Forbes has been tracking funds since 1976. They publish what they call "The Honor Roll." These funds are chosen based on the consistency and level of returns. Says *Forbes*, "An investor doesn't know when he's going to need his money and may have to cash out after less than a full market cycle. He should have some hope of keeping in the top half of the pack in fair or foul weather."* These funds have performed better than at least the top half of all mutual funds in both up and down markets. I have eliminated those funds that charge a load. You know what I think of those.

The analysis by *Forbes* determined the hypothetical after-tax return for an investor who invested $10,000 in 1976. Also shown on the chart is the weighted average price-earnings (P/E) ratio for

* "The Honor Roll," *Forbes*, September 16, 1985, pp. 80–81.

the particular portfolio and the expense per $100 in assets (see Chart 32).

CHART 32

Forbes's No-Load Honor Roll

Fund Name and Sponsor (Telex)	Nine-Year Average Annual Return	Hypothetical Investment Results*	Weighted Average P/E	Annual Expense per $100 in Assets
Acorn Fund Acorn 312-621-0630 (Call collect)	20.6%	$42,642	19.3	$0.85
Evergreen Fund Leiber & Company 800-635-0003	26.4%	$64,262	12.6	$1.10
Janus Fund Janus 800-525-3713	20.9%	$39,832	22.4	$1.06
Nicholas Fund Nicholas Company 414-272-6133	25.4%	$62,581	12.7	$0.82
Scudder Development Fund Scudder Funds 800-453-3305	20.8%	$48,041	20.0	$1.34
Tudor Fund Weiss, Peck, & Greer 800-223-3332	21.5%	$52,608	24.9	$1.59
20th Century Select 20th Century Investors 800-345-2021	28.0%	$75,952	12.6	$1.04

* Assumes $10,000 invested in 1976, after taxes.

Source: "The Honor Roll," *Forbes* (New York: Forbes, Inc.), vol. 136, no. 7, September 1985, pp. 80–81.

Now What Do You Do?

Using the phone numbers, call several funds. Choose the ones that have the lowest expenses and the highest returns. Get a prospectus sent to you, fill out the application, send a check, and you're on your way. It's really easy. Now that we've solved the "which one" issue, let's consider "when to buy."

Beat the Market or Forget Timing

Once you make the decision to go into a particular mutual fund, your next step is to decide when to buy.

As I write this the stock market has just gone through the roof. Again. During the middle part of the 1980s, the market's climb had been dramatic, unpredicted, and unprecedented. A financial planner, trying to convince me that now was the time, said, "You already missed the big climb. It's better to get in late than never." I said, "It's gone up so much already, I'm going to buy everyone else's profits. I'll be holding the bag." "No, no, no, that's not true. There's a lot of hidden value still out there," he said to me. "He might have had a point," I think to myself in retrospect.

But there is a real dilemma here. When the market's on the way up you think, "It's at the top." When the market's on the way down you think, "It's just going to keep going down." In both scenarios you convince yourself that now is not the time. Market timing—choosing the best time to get in and to get out—is a skill, an art, and an alchemy. There is one solution, however.

Dollar-cost averaging is the solution that eliminates much of the guessing. Using this investment technique with mutual funds mitigates the potential losses and enhances profit.

It's really a simple concept. Using the technique, in effect, says that instead of trying to time the market, you will go with the market. Because you're investing in no-load mutual funds, you won't incur any transaction costs. You set up a regimen to invest the same amount at regular intervals. I find that once a month, as opposed to, say, once every two months, is better because you feel as if it is a monthly charge, like your other monthly bills. Each month you invest the same amount. You buy a different number of shares each month because the price, the net asset value, has changed.

Let's say you save $100 each month. Every month, regardless of market activity, you send your mutual fund company $100. The fund management sells you the number of shares your $100 will buy at the current net asset value. To see the practical implications of this strategy, let's look at two scenarios: a falling and a rising stock price.

One scenario shows the value of your mutual fund shares dropping from $6.00 to $5.00, and the other one depicts the value of your shares appreciating from $5.00 to $6.00. In the falling-market scenario you lose $100, while in the rising-market scenario you gain $120 (see Chart 34).

CHART 33

		Dollar-Cost Average—Falling Market	
Month	Investment	Net Asset Value per Share	Number of Shares Bought
Jan.	$100	$6.00	16.67
Feb.	$100	$6.00	16.67
Mar.	$100	$6.00	16.67
Apr.	$100	$6.00	16.67
May	$100	$6.00	16.67
Jun.	$100	$6.00	16.67
Jul.	$100	$5.00	20
Aug.	$100	$5.00	20
Sep.	$100	$5.00	20
Oct.	$100	$5.00	20
Nov.	$100	$5.00	20
Dec.	$100	$5.00	20
Total	$1,200		220

Average Price Paid per Share = $5.50
Average Cost to You per Share = $1,200/200 Shares = $5.45

Dollar-Cost Average—Rising Market

Month	Investment	Net Asset Value per Share	Number of Shares Bought
Jan.	$100	$5.00	20
Feb.	$100	$5.00	20
Mar.	$100	$5.00	20
Apr.	$100	$5.00	20
May	$100	$5.00	20
Jun.	$100	$5.00	20
Jul.	$100	$6.00	16.67
Aug.	$100	$6.00	16.67
Sep.	$100	$6.00	16.67
Oct.	$100	$6.00	16.67
Nov.	$100	$6.00	16.67
Dec.	$100	$6.00	16.67
Total	$1,200		220

Average Price Paid per Share = $5.50
Average Cost to You per Share = $1,200/200 Shares = $5.45

CHART 34

	Falling Market	Rising Market
Sell on Dec. 31:	$1,100	$1,320
Basis	−$1,200	$1,200
Gain/(Loss)	− $100	120

Your average cost per share drops via dollar-cost averaging. In both cases you bought shares for an average price of $5.50, but, due to your special strategy, the average cost to you was $5.45.

You don't have to worry about market timing. You don't have to worry about which way the market's going to move tomorrow. It's not a method, though, that will lead to huge profits overnight. (This also means it's a method that will shield you from major losses overnight as well.) Over the long haul, as I suggested above, this fits into your savings and investment strategy.

In my scenarios you lost money in the down market and made

some in the up market. To highlight the actual risks and rewards inherent in the various market timing strategies, I did some further calculations, assuming that if you didn't invest the $1,200 in the mutual fund account, you'd have that money sitting in a money market fund earning 6 percent. You have four choices about how to handle that money. First, you can invest all the money in the mutual fund at the beginning of the year. Second, you can invest $600 on January 1 and $600 on June 1. Third, you can follow the dollar-cost averaging strategy discussed above. Finally, you can avoid the market altogether and simply keep the capital in the 6 percent money market fund. I assume, as I have above, that you sell your position at January 1 in the following year. Here are the results (see Chart 35):

CHART 35

Various Timing Scenarios for $1,200 Investment			
	Gain in Rising Market	Loss in Falling Market	Difference
1. Invest All in January	$240	−$200	$440
2. Invest $100 Each Month	$153	−$ 67	$220
3. Invest $600 in January and June	$138	−$ 82	$220
4. Invest in Money Market Fund	$ 66	+$ 66	0

The fourth option represents the risk-free option of letting the money sit in a money market account for the whole year.

The largest potential gain—and loss!—comes from investing all your money at the beginning of the year. This is clearly the riskiest option. You bet all your eggs that you can correctly time the market. If you're right, you come out $240 ahead. But if you're wrong, you come out $200 in the hole. This risky course highlights the wide swing between the rising market and the falling numbers returns—$440. As mentioned earlier, the highest reward is obtained at the highest risk.

The second and third options—twice a year versus each month —have the same difference in return between the rising and falling market. Their risk is roughly the same. With the dollar-cost averaging method, though, your best return is $153—$15, or 11 percent, better than the twice-a-year method. Similarly, your loss on the falling market scenario is $67—$15, or 22 percent, better than the twice-yearly scenario. In other words, with dollar-cost averaging, you minimize your risk while improving your chances for either coming out ahead or reducing the amount you might lose.

While this is a simplistic example, it highlights the advantages of dollar-cost averaging with mutual funds. You've got to tackle the market and build your own portfolio sensibly with proven strategies. And one proven strategy—we've proved it above—is that dollar-cost averaging combined with investing in mutual funds minimizes the potential for loss of capital while ensuring that slowly but surely your investment base will surge forward.

A paradox does emerge. As a buyer each month, you want the share prices to go down so you end up buying more shares. As an owner of the shares, you want the market value to go up. You root for both sides. However, from the longer-term perspective that you've adopted—you're looking for long-term capital appreciation on your investment—you really want the share value to be high just when you sell.

Wrap-up

Mutual funds can and should fit into your own personal financial investment strategy. They've been around for a long time. It's only in the last few years that they have become as easy to use as savings accounts. There's no reason you shouldn't have your investment and savings money in them. We've discussed how they operate and which you should consider. Now is the time. Call up one of those numbers provided earlier and make the leap. You can now walk confidently and calmly down Wall Street.

There is no secret. There is no formula for assured success in the stock market. That's what makes it a game. However, we can approach investing in the stock market in a manner that isn't risk-rampant. The secret of success is not the big killing. For every big killing there's someone else who's been killed. Using mutual funds to earn your portfolio a satisfactory as well as satisfying return brings to mind the old fable about the tortoise and the hare.

As you'll recall, the hare springs ahead early in the race, only to get waylaid. Meanwhile, the tortoise keeps trudging along at an even pace. The hare gets wind of this, sprints ahead, and gets sidetracked once again. The tortoise, ever mindful of his abilities —fortitude, stick-to-itiveness, and patience—and his weaknesses —feet that are too short—continues to plod along at an even pace. Finally, the tortoise crosses the finish line ahead of the hare, who has been busy playing catch-up since his last daliance with a cute little bunny. And so it is with mutual funds. They keep trudging along and win the race over the long haul.

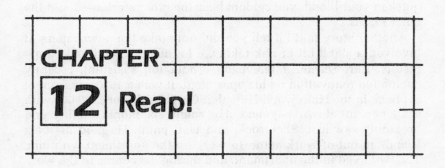

CHAPTER 12 Reap!

Business News Item:

Salomon Brothers, that solid bedrock of investment banking in New York, recently bought 30,000 three-month put options on the British pound. Acting on a client's behalf, Solly paid $1 million for the securities.* (Put options enable the holder to sell the security at a prespecified price within a certain time. The holder of a put bets that the price will tumble.)

If the price of the pound drops a mere 9.5 percent within three months, these puts will be worth $530 million. On the downside, if the pound rests in quietude, the client could be out a cool million bucks.

Think of it: $530 million. More than half a billion dollars. That's a 52,900 percent return. It's fairly risky, I'd say.

While it would certainly be nice to make that killing, I hope to have convinced you in this book that it's probably not a risk worth undertaking. Our plan does not include trading currency options. If you had taken on the British currency bet highlighted

* "Option Deal Is Largest Ever," *The New York Times* (New York: The New York Times, Inc.), October 10, 1986, p. D6.

above, you might have lost a million dollars, which might have taken you years and years—maybe a lifetime—to accumulate. While there are always exciting stories about killings that quicken your blood, you seldom hear the other stories—about the quiet losses.

Another story that I'll tell you did not make the newspapers. It involved a small bit of risk-taking, a lot of work, and had happy results. Carl Darno, a television production assistant, recently completed renovation on his apartment. It was a 1920s apartment set back in the Hollywood Hills that Carl bought for $120,000 with a 10 percent down payment. He spent six months living and breathing sawdust, Sheetrock, and wall paint. He paid his best friend, an out-of-work actor, to work on the apartment with him. The two lived in the apartment, and during the course of the work his best friend bordered on becoming his ex-best friend.

Carl had purchased the apartment as a fixer-upper. He intended to live in the apartment and then sell it once it was complete. Carl had really never undertaken such a complete overhaul as the apartment required. Walls needed to be knocked down and bathrooms rebuilt. Yet Carl believed he had the mechanical inclination and the drive to succeed at the project.

After about three months of work his best friend moved out, thereby salvaging the friendship, and Carl's girlfriend moved in. While there was still work to be done, most of the heavy work had been completed. In the next few months he finished the trim and less onerous work. In all, the project took about six months.

Just about the same time as he finished his work, he put the apartment on the market. He listed the apartment with several real estate brokers and also advertised it himself through the newspaper. He asked $190,000 for the apartment if sold through a broker or $179,000 if sold without a broker.

Typically, the broker's commission is paid by the seller. In this instance, by charging two different prices, Carl arranged for the commission to be paid by the buyer. He sold it after two months on the market. The buyer—who did not come through a broker— agreed to pay $175,000.

Carl had put down $12,000 for the apartment and had spent

$20,000 on supplies and his friend's labor. He had also paid $5,000 in lawyers fees and bank-loan fees. His total investment amounted to $37,000. For the eight-month deal he netted $34,000, a 92 percent return. The money quickly showed up back in Carl's mutual fund investments.

Carl is a real go-getter. He used to drive a Mercedes jeep—one not sold in this country. He bought it in Europe, tooled around over there, imported it to the United States, and subsequently sold it. He made a profit. Carl will be a very wealthy man some-day. He'll continue to take risks and to build up his nest egg. He's in no hurry.

Financial planning is not about making a killing overnight. It's a long process—and one that requires thought, planning, and ac-tion. My intent has been to steer you away from risky bets, to introduce you to financial thinking, and to present a guide outlin-ing how to spend and invest your money. You've learned intrica-cies, formulas, and nuances to investing wisely. We have estab-lished a framework for your own financial planning. You now have more than enough information to get on the financial steam-ship. Once aboard, you need to know how to assemble your port-folio.

Your Portfolio

You have a portfolio of assets. It ranges from your clothes, your furniture, and your house (if you own one) to your stocks, mutual funds, and IRA's to the cash you keep in your wallet. Where you choose to keep it, in what kinds of accounts and investment vehi-cles, is a function of your needs and your own preferences. You need to keep money so you have access to it for day-to-day needs, and that's why you probably have a checking or NOW account. You should also hold money in an account that will ap-preciate considerably. At the farthest point on this liquidity scale is your IRA investment. You won't touch your IRA until you're fifty-nine and a half years old. Accordingly, this asset money is not liquid.

You already have established certain "risk parameters" within your portfolio. Your aim is to develop a portfolio consistent with your desires. Clearly, your checking account money *must* be there. Hence, your risk tolerance for checking-account needs is low. For your savings and investment account, you can accept more risk in the sense that the rate of return can fluctuate. With this money you can afford to be a little more adventurous. That is, it isn't required for your day-to-day needs or even your annual needs. Finally, the money in your individual retirement account (IRA), your company pension plan, your KEOGH account, or any other long-term savings vehicle, should be invested in a riskier venture. You can't touch it for at least another twenty years and you might as well seek capital appreciation or growth. This last suggestion wouldn't be appropriate if you were approaching retirement. However, at the beginning of your financial career, you can afford to consider slightly riskier investments.

The general notion is that, depending on your needs for each kind of monetary holding, you can establish different risk parameters. Since at this stage of your financial career you can afford to take on riskier investments, my general suggestion is that the less you need the money, the more adventurous you should be in investing it. (I don't mean options, though.) Put your pension or long-term savings into a risky asset—an aggressive growth fund or a highly leveraged investment fund. For your investment account, place your funds in a growth equity fund. For your checking account, open a checking account that pays interest.

This isn't to say, however, you should invest in a computer and establish mathematically precise risk-return parameters. The intent is to give you a feel for categorizing your assets among investments involving varying degrees of risk.

This is the nutshell of risk and return, the central nucleus of investing. Any time you convert income to an income-producing asset, you face these questions: How much will it go up? How much do I stand to lose? With the lower-risk investments, you can easily find out. But with higher-risk investments, those that offer the potential of higher returns, you can't know. That's the central maxim. The greater the uncertainty, the higher amount the asset should promise you in return. Options and futures involve the greatest volatility, the greatest potential for an entire loss of your money, but they also offer the tremendous opportunity to triple, quadruple, quintuple, or the next -tuple your money.

Throughout your investing life keep in the back—and certainly in the front—of your mind that you want to maximize return, minimize risk, and understand the potential components every time you make an investment decision. If, as is the central concept behind financial planning, you convert income into assets, you want to make sure that you'll have greater wealth available for yourself in the future.

The Steps Revisited

After having gone through these chapters and exercises, you will be able to diagram your overriding financial strategy. To repeat, though, achieving your financial goals will not be hard and can be accomplished. You need diligence to follow through with the steps:

1. Make a Plan.
2. Save Creatively.
3. Buy a Home.
4. Invest.

In the preceding chapters I have presented many stories of young people who by and large have been relatively successful in their ventures. I did not include the stories of some phenomenally successful people because, while it is nice if you strike it rich, you shouldn't count on it. In fact, those people who by luck of the market did make a killing had not really planned on it.

The one thought that I was left with after conducting interviews was the perseverance that the many people highlighted in this book exhibited. You have to want to build your nest egg. You have to want to work at saving your money. You have to want a house. All this requires work and dedication. The one message I hope you have gained from this book is that you can achieve financial success. All you have to do is work at it.